FLOWER ARRANGEMENTS
FOR SPECIAL OCCASIONS

An arrangement for a christening in a shallow heart-shaped dish with a cherub, using only wild flowers. Daisies and cow parsley

Flower Arrangements for Special Occasions

Winifrede Morrison

Drawings by Margaret Davies

B. T. Batsford Ltd London

For Janet and Susan, with love
and to help with the parties
given for Mark, Claire, Ruth,
Daisy and Sam

© Winifrede Morrison 1976
First published 1976

ISBN 0 7134 3088 5

Filmset by
Servis Filmsetting Ltd, Manchester
Printed in Great Britain by
The Anchor Press Ltd, Tiptree, Essex
for the publishers B. T. Batsford Ltd
4 Fitzhardinge Street,
London W1H 0AH

Contents

Acknowledgment

To my husband for help with the typing and some of the photographs, Margaret Davies for the drawings and Frank Martin for the remainder of the photographs.

Introduction

Most of the ideas in this book are designed for use by those who have some knowledge of flower arrangement, so few basic principles are included. But, on the other hand, many suggestions could be carried out quite easily by anyone who has never 'arranged' a flower; the chapters for children's parties are a case in point.

All of the ideas are basically merely suggestions which it is hoped may trigger off new inspirations in different styles. After all, most creative ideas are essentially individual; and if those I have described here inspire my readers I shall have had not only pleasure from creating and writing about them, but an extra – if unknown – reward.

A home-made cradle for a christening, filled with tiny flowers, including lily-of-the-valley, pinks, wild marguerites and cow parsley

christenings

In the home

All white flowers, pale blue or pale pink – or a mixture of each. Pink and blue can be combined for twins (if there is one of each!). Suitable containers: Cupids, silver dishes, delicate glass – or make a cradle.

To make a cradle

Material required: a small plastic, cardboard or wicker dish which has held fruit, cress or similar items, (an oval or oblong shape is best). Some pieces of fabric, odd bits of nylon, lace or whatever comes to hand. A piece of thin cardboard to bend into a half circle to make the hood.

Cover the cardboard hood with the chosen fabric – all the fabric can be glued on as this is quick and easy. The container is a very temporary thing and need not be too carefully finished off. Glue or staple the cardboard, at both sides, to one end of the dish to make the hood. Now cut a piece of material about one and a half times the total outside measurement of the dish, and about 1-in (2·5cm) deeper. Make a hem at both sides and glue this down. When it is dry, run a thread through the top and gather it together until it fits around the dish. Glue or tape it to the edge.

Put a piece of well-soaked plastic foam wrapped in silver foil (wrong side out, it is not so shiny) inside and fill it with dainty flowers and foliage. Or place a small baby doll inside and cover the foam with flower heads so that it looks like a coverlet. A tinier version could also be made to go on the top of the christening cake.

Silver spoons can be used too – perhaps one at each place. A small piece of foam in the bowl of the spoon takes a tiny arrangement, plus a ribbon bow.

Another idea is to line bootees or babies shoes with foil and foam and to do an arrangement in these.

A delicate and unusual effect for a table-centre arrangement is to stand three containers, say wide wine glasses, inside each other in a pyramid style. Line one glass with foil and a ring of foam, anchor the next inside this and put the third one on top. Arrange flowers and small foliage in each one.

I feel that small unsophisticated flowers are most suitable for this occasion – Forget-me-nots, tiny border pinks, Carole roses, daisies, the side shoots of delphiniums or spray chrysanthemums. But when these are not obtainable, dried and dyed plant material can be used.

A cone of 'Doris' pinks and lily-of-the-valley for a christening. MARGARET HALL

Helichrysums and helipterums come in pale pinks and white, and some Statice in a blueish shade.

It is also possible to obtain very pretty colours by home dyeing. Use an ordinary hot-water dye – I use *Dylon* – and, for this purpose, make the pale blue or pink mixture fairly weak. Dip the natural coloured material in the hot dye for a few seconds only, then leave to dry. Don't worry if it looks bedraggled, it will come up beautifully. Hare's tail grasses, Statice, pampas grass and many bleached ferns are dainty and will take colour very well.

Make a wreath for the door, on the same principles as for Christmas, but with light foliage and pink and blue flowers. A lovely start to a party! Make, too, a little posy to hang on the cradle or pram. And why not a special corsage for the new mother?

A table design in a basket, in pale pink and blue, for a christening

The church

Be very careful about Church flowers and always consult the authorities first.

Obviously it is important not to overcrowd the font on this occasion and it may be difficult to decorate the top. If this is attempted, be sure to leave room for the officiating clergyman to reach inside the font. A small shallow tin at each corner could be the answer, or the base can be decorated – though this is hidden when people gather round it. One pretty idea is to make small semi-Victorian posies, each one placed inside a silver cake doiley, with the stems cut quite short and inserted into foil covered foam. These can be attached at strategic places with sticky tape.

Do remember to concentrate the arrangements near the font which is the focus on this occasion. A pedestal in white flowers is always lovely if the font presents too many difficulties – but do use simple and unsophisticated flowers.

A font decorated for the christening of twins, in pale blue, pink and white. BARBARA NORTH

Birthdays

Children of all ages enjoy a festive table on their birthday, so make it look rather special with some of the following ideas:

Children's parties

Roundabout

Material required: A flat round piece of wood about 1-in (2cm) thick and 30-in (76cm) in diameter; five wooden rods, or pieces of dowelling about 8-in (20cm) high; thin cardboard; paint; oasis; round shallow tin for flowers.

Fix the rods firmly to the base either by screwing them in or using a strong glue in a hole drilled half-way through the base. Cut the cardboard a little larger than the base (about 2-in, 5cm, larger) and mark it in wedges radiating from the centre like a tent top. Paint these in two colours – one in each alternate wedge – and leave a plain wedge at one end to overlap. There has to be an even number of colour wedges so that the same colour doesn't come together when the completed top is glued. Cut another strip of cardboard about 2-in (5cm) wide and scallop it at one edge. Glue the straight edge underneath the large circle and bend the scalloped piece downwards to make a frill.

Now fix this into a cone shape, not too elongated, either with staples or sticky tape. Arrange matching flowers in the wet oasis in the round shallow tin. Bring the flowers well outside the base in

A roundabout in red and yellow, filled with flowers, for a children's party

*How to construct a roundabout
to take flowers for a party*

places to avoid a flat look. Put on the cardboard top, securing this also with sticky tape.

A sugar animal made of marzipan or chocolate could also be placed at the base of each rod; or, if there are more children than rods, at intervals on the edge of the rondabout. Or real 'Magic Roundabout' figures, of course.

Perhaps this all sounds rather complicated, but the drawings will show how easy it really is.

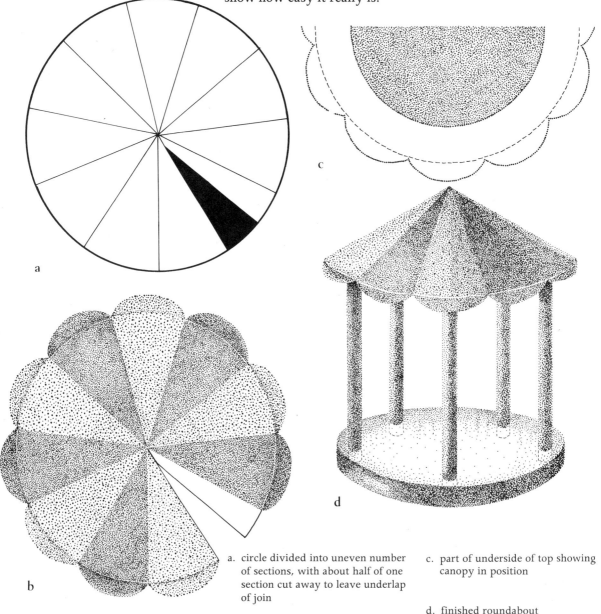

a. circle divided into uneven number of sections, with about half of one section cut away to leave underlap of join

b. upper side of top with scalloped edge and even number of sections painted in alternate colours

c. part of underside of top showing canopy in position

d. finished roundabout

Womble Party

A very simple idea for a Womble party would be to find a flat round basket for the centre of the table. Arrange some wild flowers in a tall container (smaller in diameter) and place this in the centre of the basket. Wrap up the presents in odd scraps of torn paper or newspaper and pile them in the basket, making them look as much like 'litter' as possible. Some real Womble figures dotted about would make this even better.

The Owl and the Pussycat

Use either a boat-shaped container or an oval dish and place this on a long thin board covered in sea-blue fabric or crepe paper. Make a thin cardboard sail for the boat before filling it with whatever flowers are available. Pop a toy owl and a cat at either end – one of them could be sitting on a jar of honey. Add some foil-covered chocolate money (if you can find it, of course!) and a toy guitar.

Parcel

Wrap a large box with gay paper; stripes or plain colours are best for this. Place ribbon round the parcel and a small tinfoil dish filled with oasis in the centre. Do an arrangement in this, picking up the colours of the ribbon and paper. Fix ribbon streamers to flow out from the centre arrangement to each place. Wrap small gifts in matching colours and attach these to the place-ends of the streamers.

Cinderella Scene

This can be staged on an oblong board, covered half in pale pink and half in hessian. Or brown and pink crepe paper could be used. Make a very dainty fresh arrangement and try to repeat it as nearly as possible in a dried arrangement for the other end. Link the two with a small gourd (for the pumpkin), a tiny broomstick made from twigs, a small silver slipper (the decorative kind used for wedding cakes), and place a watch with hands at midnight in the centre.

Sleeping Beauty

This can be done in a very similar way, simply by varying the accessories: omit the gourd, slipper and watch and substitute a tiny spinning wheel in the centre. These can be found in the shops but could also be made fairly easily. The wheel doesn't have to be too authentic – a painted cardboard disc would do at a pinch. Link this theme up with cobwebs – strands of 'angel's hair' (which is available at Christmas) would do; or make cobwebs from fine fuse wire.

Swan Lake

Use any mirror for the base. Put foil underneath to protect the table, and surround the mirror edge with moss or soaked foam. Tuck small flowers into the moss and put a very delicate white arrangement in the centre. Glass or white china swans dotted here and there make it very appealing for a child who likes ballet.

Rainbow Table

Cut a long fairly wide half-circle of pliable cardboard and paint it in strips of rainbow colours. Attach it to the side of the table with sticky tape and do a flower arrangement in the centre in the same colours. Fix ribbon streamers to the rainbow, one to each place, with a bag of gold chocolate coins at the ends.

Teenagers' Parties

This covers such a wide field – a thirteen-year-old may not like the same things when he or she is nineteen! However, perhaps some of the ideas could be adapted accordingly.

Thirteen would possibly be a girls-only affair, and one pretty idea is to make a very flat arrangement in the centre of the table. Try to get the flowers into circles rather like a Victorian posy; it will be helpful to use wire mesh or soaked foam for this. Surround the finished design with a paper cake doiley, in white and silver, and take ribbon streamers out from this to each place. Repeat the arrangement in miniature at each place setting, using perhaps a cut-down cream or yoghurt pot so that the guests can take them home.

Older teenagers might like a more vivid design: any old 78 gramophone record can be moulded into a container which would be suitable for this. Plug the centre with foil and use soaked foam for the flowers.

Some of the ideas under "Coming-of-age" might also be used for a teenage party.

Coming-of-age

I do not think that the old themes of keys and so on are suitable nowadays, so maybe it is as well to keep the flowers for this occasion as simple as possible. For a girl, the colours of her dress could be considered, and of course her personal tastes. For a man, vivid colours arranged in metals – brass, copper, pewter – look most effective; and some of the party ideas for taking streamers and favours to each place could be included.

Any special interest can also be incorporated. I once did a group of small flower balls in the colours of a football club, surrounding a larger ball. I'm sure the guests enjoyed them even if they did end up by playing rounders! A buffet lends itself to the interpretative type of arrangement rather better than a set table where there is not always enough room for a bit of floral nonsense.

Consider the miniature items in a toy shop, such as guitars, tambourines and racquets. None of these is very expensive, and they lend themselves to all kinds of designs simply by the addition of some wrapped foil to hold the flowers. Much better to think up something which is fun and a talking-point than to use precious containers and expensive flowers.

I did a coming-of-age party once to harmonize with a lovely cyclaman-coloured dress – not easy to match in flowers. I used various shades of pink, ranging from pale to dark; this broke up the sombre colours and had the added advantage of disguising the fact that there was not much exactly-matching colour. Pink and red pyrethrums, sweet williams in various colours, pink tulips, roses, ixias (which matched the dress exactly). And, as it was a country party, field marguerites and Queen Anne's lace to lighten the design, along with masses of lilies-of-the-valley. Long low flat arrangements for the tables and two asymmetrical designs to stand on either side of the cake. A tall cider bottle with a large round base went well on the buffet table; it contained red peonies and grapes.

The wild material needed careful preparation so I steeped the cut ends in boiling water for about ten seconds before giving them a long drink in deep water. After this, it lasted even longer than the florist's flowers! Queen Anne's lace is invaluable material when available – so light and dainty and exquisite in any arrangement.

Parties

Luncheon

Simple designs are usually the best for these parties: checked cloths, coarse linen, hessian or a bare table with straw mats make the nicest setting for flowers in a basket or a heavy pottery container. One of the tall green cider bottles with a squat base is attractive, too, and garden flowers look good in all these containers.

A simple basket can be made at home. Put a flat piece of soaked foam in a foil dish and wire a hoop of cane or straw (if available) to look like a basket handle. If there is nothing else, wire could be used and covered with crepe paper or ribbon. Bring the flowers well out over the edges; this not only hides the foil dish but avoids a flat look.

Colours can be taken right through both the flowers and the food, and because it is a daylight occasion, blue could be used. (Blue and lilac are not good colours for artificial light at night.) Any creamy mousse can be changed to blue with vegetable colouring, either as a starter or a dessert, though it may be a little harder to think of a main course in blue! However, if you remember that the colouring is harmless, anything is possible.

Remember, too, that it is possible to dye an old white tablecloth and napkins for a particular colour scheme.

Table setting for an informal summer lunch, with cardboard plates and paper napkins on a green cloth. Pink flowers in a copper jug

18

Tea

Arrangements for tea parties need to be rather small and light, although always in proportion to the table and space available. There are so many pretty paper cloths and napkins now that the scope is enormous.

Unless it is a very formal tea, garden flowers look nicest, but I have seen a mixture of lily-of-the-valley and Queen Anne's lace arranged on a white lace table-cloth which looked absolutely lovely.

On one occasion I arranged the tiny Cecile Brunner rose in a pottery figure and placed a small group of these on each plate of food. The china also had a rose pattern which added considerably to the general effect.

Dinner

Anyone lucky enough to possess a round table can make a delightful setting for a dinner party, although most of the ideas can be adapted to fit any shape.

Make sure that the tablecloth, napkins, china and flowers make a harmonious colour scheme. For a round table, a low circular arrangement looks good. Fix wide ribbon streamers from the centre, radiating to each place setting, and put small posies for the women guests and button-holes for the men.

A candelabra can be used for dinner parties providing it is not too dense and guests are able to see through and across it. One way of achieving this is to put flowers into only one of the candle holders (with a special candle-cup) and to use candles in the others. If the flower arrangement is taken 'through' the spaces, the candles can still be lit.

Another idea with a candlestick is to use all the places for candles but to surround the base with a small ring of flowers. Protect the table with foil before placing a ring of well-soaked foam for the flowers. Alternatively, the ring of flowers can be used just underneath the candle itself; and if the plant material has been well conditioned it could be pushed into a ring of wire alone. It will certainly last the length of a dinner party, even with the candles alight.

Although lovely dishes can be used, an equally attractive dinner party arrangement can be done in any low container, even a foil dish. Remember the shape of the table all the time. An oblong table looks best with a long low arrangement; a square table can take this shape too, placed straight or across at an angle. A really square shape would not look very interesting, though there is no reason why a round or oval shape should not go on a square table. Do sit down and look at the arrangement before leaving it. It is rather irritating to find in the middle of dinner that there is a large 'hole' in front of your most important guest!

Straw basket of wild roses, suitable for a garden party.
BARBARA NORTH

Garden

When planning decorations for a garden party there are several things to remember which might not immediately spring to mind. The cloth and the container need to be heavy in weight, because parties in the garden are subject to sudden changes in weather – and the least of the worries is to rescue the flowers!

Baskets are very suitable as long as they are sturdy ones, a trug for instance. Keep the arrangements as low as possible (again because of winds) and take into consideration the garden itself. If it is a very green garden, make the scheme vivid and striking. An old white sheet could go first on the table and then one of the bright paper ones; tape or weight this down, and use simple china. A linen or hessian cloth looks well with *wooden* plates and bowls.

If the table is near a flower bed, be careful not to use plant material which is going to fight with the contents of the bed; in fact, use similar material if possible, though of course no-one wants to rob the border too heavily before a party. A prolific use of fruit and vegetables is a good idea for a garden party; indeed, the first course could be raw vegetable platter (assiette de Crudités). Pile groups of carrots, cucumber, celery, radishes, tomatoes, any of the green salad family, mushrooms, avocado, etc., in a large wooden bowl. Make sure they are all well cleaned beforehand, of course, and add some colourful graters by the side so that guests can choose and prepare their own, plus a good dressing or mayonnaise.

At the other end of the table pile another bowl with as many fruits as available. Both these bowls will not only look attractive but make interesting and easy first and last courses. And there can still be a flower arrangement in the centre so that the table does not look too bare at the end of the party.

Supper

This demands a more informal scheme of decoration; one idea is to use the little candle lanterns which are available. A ring of flowers can be placed at the base outside the lantern and, if the colour of the candle is picked up in the flowers, it will look very pretty. Of course, the candle can be dispensed with altogether and a posy of flowers put inside the lantern.

Think about having flowers at one end of the table only, in a candelabra for instance. It keeps them well away from the food. Also remember that most supper parties will be late-ish and by artificial light except for mid-summer, so be careful about the flower colours. Lilacs, violets and blues do not show to their best advantage by night.

For a supper party which has to be prepared well in advance, a small *pot et fleur* is a suggestion. Place two or three small house-plants in a pretty dish or a basket and hide the edges of the pots with moss. Put a small piece of soaked foam between one of the

pots and, at the last minute, tuck a few fresh flowers into this. Take a pile of luscious fruits (which can also be used for dessert) and hide a small pinholder in a dish or well-pinholder to take a few flowers in the same colours as the fruit. Just three carnations or one lovely rose look attractive this way.

Buffet

Flowers for a buffet party need to be eye-catching and it is wise to make the colour scheme rather bold. The containers must be tall and well above the food so they should be sited at the back of the table. If no tall containers are available raise the height of whatever there is with boxes. Cover the boxes in the same colour as the cloth (crepe paper will do for this) and anchor the whole arrangement very firmly indeed. If raised boxes are used, anchor the container to these, too.

If people are helping themselves the problem is a lot easier, but if there is service from behind the table, limit the number of arrangements. Pity the poor waiter who is serving salads and finds he has included a trail of ivy!

Use one or two really vivid arrangements, in candle-sticks or bottles, kept rather tall and narrow, with perhaps a pyramid of fruit in the centre which can be eaten by the guests (be careful not to include plastic grapes!).

Extra interest can be given to a buffet table by placing very small posies of flowers actually on the plates of food, or by decorating the front of the table with swags of foliage. Make sure that this is fixed on with sticky tape or sewn, as pins can damage a dress very easily. I do not feel it is worth using elaborate flowers for the front of a buffet table because they are only seen to advantage when the room is empty. They become masked when people arrive and completely hidden when the meal begins. Incidentally, a small extra side table can be provided for a buffet by using an ironing-board.

Festivals

Guy Fawkes Day

Principally an outdoor party for the children, I suppose; but maybe after the bonfire has died down, the hot chocolate has been drunk and the last squib spluttered to a finish, the adults might like to retire from the cold damp world of November to a cosy bonfire night supper indoors.

It will obviously be an informal affair, with trousers and gumboots the order of the day, so neither flowers nor food should be too elaborate.

If there are still some dahlias about, these are ideal because of their vivid colouring. Use flame red and orange with some slim bullrushes to look like fireworks. Or just a very few scarlet carnations with some blackened driftwood. Set these on a black cloth for maximum effect, and serve steaming hot punch made with red wine.

Recipe for hot punch
  (Quantities according to number of people)
  4 parts cheap red wine
  1 part cider
  1 part orange squash
  1 part lemon squash
  1 orange stuck with cloves
  1 part brandy (added at the last minute)

I sometimes add a little sherry or almost anything else left at the bottom of a bottle. Of course, the mixture has to be sampled frequently to see that the proportions are right! Mix everything except the brandy and heat until almost – but not quite – boiling. Add the brandy and serve. Will keep out any cold – and make the flowers look even lovelier!

Hallowe'en

Use similar colours to the Guy Fawkes suggestions, but make liberal use of gourds. The small round ones can be made into candle-holders by gouging out the centre. Apples, too, make splendid candle-holders; but be sure for these ideas to anchor both the underneath base and the candle with plasticine for security.

Or an arrangement can be done in a marrow or a pumpkin. Scoop out a large piece from the centre and line it with foil and soaked

St Valentine's party. A home-made heart using wire coat-hangers with small flowers in wet, foil wrapped foam. Lily-of-the-valley, violets, heather

foam. Make sure the base of this is firmly on the table with foil underneath to protect the table surface.

If a cauldron type of container can be found, so much the better. Make a witch to go with this by using a cardboard cylinder from a roll of lavatory paper and black crepe paper. Just cut a cape and hood from the crepe paper, stuff the hood with more crepe paper and glue the cape round the cylinder. It doesn't have to be too exact and is simple to do. Make a little broom with twigs.

For a Hallowe'en party for children, extend the 'witch' theme. Cover the table with red crepe paper (but watch the dye if it gets wet) or silver foil, and cut out a lot more witches to scatter around. Make a hanging mobile by attaching each figure to a piece of cotton and hanging them from the ceiling. Use *Bluetack* to attach them to the ceiling or walls since this leaves no marks. Make a paper mask for each child by cutting round the shape of a pair of spectacles and sewing elastic to the edges.

St Valentine's Day

Perhaps not many people celebrate this occasion but it could be an excuse for a romantic table setting, especially for two.

Delicate pastel shades look very pretty – perhaps lilac and pale lemon? It is not necessary to have elaborate containers or candlesticks.

For a fairly large table, use one of the cheap metal coat-hangers, take off the hook then bend the wire into a heart shape. Moss, collected in the country, can be pressed into tight wads and wrapped round the coat-hanger with reel wire to secure it. If something smaller is required, or if no moss is available, well-soaked foam wrapped in foil will do. Put some extra foil underneath to protect the table before forming the foam into a heart shape in the table centre.

A plain white cloth will do but it would look even nicer if a small lace one was placed on top. Alternatively, cut out a heart from silver or gold foil, or crepe paper, slightly larger than the foam ring and use this as a base. Gold hearts can be bought from some good shops, too. *Paperchase* in Tottenham Court Road in London sometimes have them. Use two more hearts as place mats and make small napkin rings from a piece of cardboard. Cover these to match the colour scheme and stick a miniature heart on each.

Now fill the foam ring with small flowers – snowdrops, violets, primroses and heather should be available at this time of year and perhaps a few hellebores. Group tiny flowers like violets and primroses together with an elastic band before inserting them into the ring. This makes it easier to get them in as the stems are very brittle, and it looks more effective. Trails of small-leaved ivy make suitable foliage.

If the ring is large enough to take candles at intervals, insert these by making three small hairpins of wire (*see 'More ideas' chapter*).

Mother's Day

This is essentially a day for the children to give or make their own arrangements; and, as the price of flowers seems to rocket at this time, the ideas must be simple and inexpensive.

Yoghurt or cream pots can be painted or covered with paper and filled with small flowers. Children may not get on very well with foam, so try to find some moss for them to use. Any kind of shell makes a pretty container; tins or little boxes can be covered with fabric then lined with foil or polythene before being filled with flowers.

A very simple *pot et fleur* could be made with just one plant in a cheap plastic bowl with a few fresh flowers tucked inside a tiny container also in the bowl, plus a bow of ribbon.

Now that so many pretty colours are available in tissue paper, an ordinary bunch of flowers can be made to look much more festive by using this with matching ribbon. An attractive card to go with this could be made by the method described in the chapter on 'Junior Christmas'.

I do feel that a gift on this day is extra welcome if most of the effort has been made by the giver. If the children are going to take breakfast to mother in her room, then a little posy on the tray would be a nice offering.

In the United States, this special day (the second Sunday in May) a white carnation is the traditional ornament for mothers; older children may be able to make this up as described in the chapter on Floristry.

Burns' Night Supper

As Burns' Night comes in January it is not a very easy time for fresh flowers. Perhaps a combination of fresh and dried would be the answer. Say dried thistle heads, a nice piece of gnarled wood, moss and – an essential touch – some winter heather. Heathers are grown to bloom all the year round now so it should be possible to find some. If not, there is always potted heather available in January.

Design the arrangement to stand on a piece of plaid or tweed. It would be a subtle touch to incorporate a miniature set of bagpipes, a small sporran or a dirk. Another suggestion is to use an (empty) bottle of Scotch whisky and to do an arrangement in the top of this, either in plasticine (if it is dried) or in a bottle-holder fixed to the top.

Harvest Festival

I am not concerned here with the decoration of the church; that is usually a tradition special to each building and ably carried out by the ladies on the flower rota. But I do offer some suggestions for a harvest supper, either on a large scale in the village hall or at home.

Table arrangements could be done in wicker cornucopias usually used for hanging plants, if there are any available. But a scooped-out marrow, pumpkin or a long, plaited loaf are equally suitable.

Line the scooped-out hole with foil and put in a piece of soaked foam. Do a vivid arrangement, incorporating corn, fruit and vegetables. Cones, berries and seedheads should also be included. Any of the fruit can be inserted in the foam by impaling it on a wooden cocktail stick. If a touch of red is required, scarlet anemones will look very much like poppies. Other ideas for containers include any kind of basket, wooden mugs, copper or brass kettles or jugs; if an attractive pair of scales is at hand, do flowers on one side and fruit or vegetables on the other.

Personally I like to see a harvest scheme in shades of Autumn golds and yellows, but this is by no means obligatory. I feel it has to have more of the old-fashioned flowers and nothing too sophisticated; dahlias and chrysanthemums seem just right. Trails of wild clematis (Old Man's Beard) could link the arrangements if the table is a long one.

For a village hall, try to get sheaves of corn. Many farmers will keep a little corn back from the combine harvester if they are asked in time. If you can find some non-plastic milk churns, replace the lid and wire foam to take flowers in this. Old wooden yokes are still around in some country districts, and a dried arrangement wired to this and hung looks lovely. Plaques for the walls can be made by wiring fruit, seedheads, vegetables and cones onto baskets or trays.

American festivals

Flower arranging in the United States of America has reached a very high level of skill and ingenuity, and I would not presume to offer ideas to the many talented arrangers in that country. The suggestions which follow are intended to help other arrangers who might want to surprise and please their American guests.

The scope is endless: Carnation Day in Ohio; Daffodil festivals in Washington State; apple blossom and cherry blossom festivals; Rose Day in Manheim, Penn; and the fabulous Tournament of Roses in Pasedena at New Year. Dates for these can be found in *The American Book of Days* by George W. Douglas or *Festivals USA* by Robert Meyer Jnr. This latter book also details the special flower adopted by each State; a delightful idea – how nice it would be to have this for each County in Britain! It would be a great compliment to an American guest to decorate the table, or her room, with flowers representing her home State.

Among the main dates which might call for special decorations, we think first of Thanksgiving Day (the fourth Thursday in November) and Independence Day, July 4th. I had some American friends for dinner on Independence Day and I thought it might be a rather wry touch to decorate the table with the Stars and Stripes. I put a well-soaked oblong block of foam in foil and arranged a pattern of stars and stripes in flower heads. Streamers of red, white and blue ribbon went from this to each place; and, for a bit of extra fun, I stood tiny Union Jacks by the wine glasses.

St Patrick's Day is quite a celebration in New York City – all the white carnations get dyed green. Veterans Day on the fourth Monday in October is rather like Remembrance Day in Britain, so poppies are used. Of course, at this time they have to be artificial, but really lovely poppies can be made from crepe paper. For Thanksgiving in November a collection of Fall leaves arranged in a pumpkin would be a very suitable decoration.

Easter

There are two ways of using floral interpretations for Easter. One is to interpret the religious festival and the other to include all the fun things such as bonnets and eggs.

Arrangements for Church could start with an interpretation of Good Friday. A piece of blackened wood in the form of a cross, or a chaplet of thorns combined with blood-red roses or carnations would suggest itself. The arrangements for Easter Day need to be fairly tailored; I feel that lots of fussy white flowers are not right for this occasion – lilies are most suitable. Five arums, with their own foliage, arranged in a curve either side of the altar cross look beautiful. It is easy to bend arum stems if a tiny piece of the fleshy stem is peeled-off right the way down, then the stem stroked very gently between the thumb and first finger. (Daffodils can be 'stroked' into shape, too). Cut the stem to the length required, then bind round the cut end with wool, otherwise it is likely to split when impaled on a pinholder.

Baskets of spring flowers near the font, and in the Church windows, and a tailored pedestal of green and white or yellow and white. If Easter is late enough to include some blossom, this too looks lovely arranged in huge sprays in a stone urn.

An idea for the children: take the shell from your breakfast egg with about two-thirds left intact. Cut the edge very carefully into points with small sharp-pointed scissors. Secure it on a piece of plasticine so that it stands firmly, then fill the shell with soil and sprinkle on some grass seed. Now paint a face on the outside and it will, eventually, have green hair! Or paint a pretty pattern on the shell and put some tiny flowers, primroses perhaps, in between the grass as a gift.

All kinds of extravaganza are permissible in the home at Easter but the flowers should be kept as simple as possible. Early tulips, grape hyacinths, daffodils, primroses, violets and catkins with pussy willow and all sorts of accessories can be used.

Cardboard eggs make good containers, but be sure to attach a small wedge of plasticine underneath so that they stand firmly. Line the egg with foil or polythene and then some wet oasis. It is possible to attach the top half, also with plasticine, so that it appears as though the flowers are arranged in a half-open basket. This looks very pretty. Wicker eggs are sometimes available and, if there is time and inclination, an egg may be made from papier mache and painted to the required colour. Add a little fluffy yellow chicken,

A Show design interpretating Easter, using arum lilies against a pale yellow drape

a lamb made from pipe-cleaners, or an Easter bunny for the children.

A small bird's nest placed on a piece of wood can be filled with tiny sugar eggs and combined with either a little arrangement placed at the side, or with daffodils and pussy willow. It is often possible to find a discarded nest or to make one from moss and twigs.

A table arrangement in an oval shape is pretty at this time, especially if done in a fairly wide dish so that some foil-wrapped eggs can be tucked in at the sides. The attractive china chickens which are in the shops now make delightful focus points for an Easter design. Give the chicken a flowery mat to sit on by placing first a large piece of foil; cover this with moss and perch the chicken in the centre. Then tuck small Spring flowers around – primroses, violets or anything small which is available. Fill the chicken with candy eggs.

An Easter bunny. Small pink roses and lily-of-the-valley in a white jar, with a china rabbit attached to the side with cement solution

Another idea is to make an Easter bonnet of flowers. For this I use one of the old-fashioned round white electric light shades, in opaque or white glass. Stand this, upside down, on a round board. I secure mine with a ring of plasticine for safety. As I am not good at drawing faces, I simply paint on some long curly eyelashes, which gives a very coy effect, and a red mouth. If there is an old hat available, so much the better; but, if not, use a round foil container or make a brim from soft cardboard. Put a round of well-soaked oasis in the centre and arrange flowers covering the centre of the 'hat'. Secure the container to the china shade with sticky tape – and there's the Easter bonnet.

A word here about conditioning Spring flowers: *daffodils* prefer to stand in a small amount of water once they have been conditioned in deep water for several hours; *violets* require surface spraying – and be careful here because they are apt to siphon water out through the petals on to a table surface; *anemones* are not very happy in foam, though they may do better if a hole is made first for the stems so that they do not become clogged with the foam; *tulips* need to be wrapped completely in newspaper and put up to their necks in water before use – and, of course, cut a small portion from every stem before conditioning.

Christmas

Christmas is a time to relax all the rules usually applied to flower arranging, to use plastic, paint, glitter and many kinds of different artificial material. For one thing, this is economical because fresh flowers are expensive; another very important reason is that artificial decorations can be made well ahead, whenever there is some spare time before the rush of Christmas starts in earnest.

But for those who do not like paint and glitter, I would suggest artificial flowers arranged with real foliage. It is possible to make carnations and roses which will deceive the most critical eye, as I will show. Most of these ideas are not expensive or too difficult to make. And, as Christmas is the children's time, I have included some simple ideas for them to try.

Paper Flowers

Ranunculas
Material required: Scarlet crepe paper; orange crepe paper; stub
    wires 22 (0·71mm) or 24 gauge (0·56mm); small black beads or
    seed-heads for centres; florist's tape or crepe paper
    Cut circles of crepe paper about 2-in (5cm) in diameter. Each
flower requires 26 scarlet and five orange circles. Thread them all
onto a stub wire, starting with scarlet and interspersing the orange
ones here and there, irregularly. Put a bead or small seed-head on
the top of the wire and bend it into a tiny hairpin to secure it firmly.
Push the circles tightly together at the top and cover the stub wire
with tape or crepe paper. Twist this around several times at the top
to prevent the circles slipping down.

Water lilies
Material required: Cardboard or polystyrene apple cartons (the
    kind with a shape for each apple); seed-head for centre; strong
    stub wires 26 gauge (0·46mm); florist's tape
    Cut around the apple shapes so that it is a large petal shape.
Each flower takes five or six petals. Push a stub wire through the
base of each petal. Thread a bead or seed-head on another stub wire,
then wire the petals around this, facing inwards.

Carnations

Material required: Large paper napkin with dull surface. (One
   napkin makes two flowers); stub wires 24 gauge (0·56mm);
   florist's tape or crepe paper

With the napkin in a square, cut off the patterned edge. Unfold
the square to a rectangle, then re-fold it the other way so that there
is a strip measuring about 12-in (30cm) long and 4-in (10cm)
wide. Cut along both edges of this with pinking shears to make a
serrated edge. Divide into two and pleat one strip tightly together
until it is a concertina-like wedge. Bind a stub wire very tightly
round the centre, then start to tease out the layers of paper between
your fingers. There are usually four very thin layers and great care
is necessary so as not to tear the paper. Now push the whole thing
up from underneath to make a flower. The wire stem can be taped,
covered with a strip of crepe paper or put on a false stem.

Use scarlet napkins for Christmas, of course; though very pretty
effects can be obtained for other occasions by trying pastel shades.

Combine these flowers with ivy, cupresses or almost any evergreen and they look really lovely, especially in a pedestal.

How to make a paper carnation

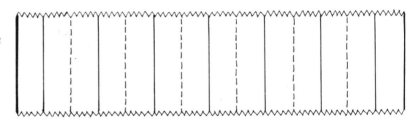

Strip showing position of folds

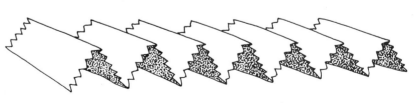

folded strip

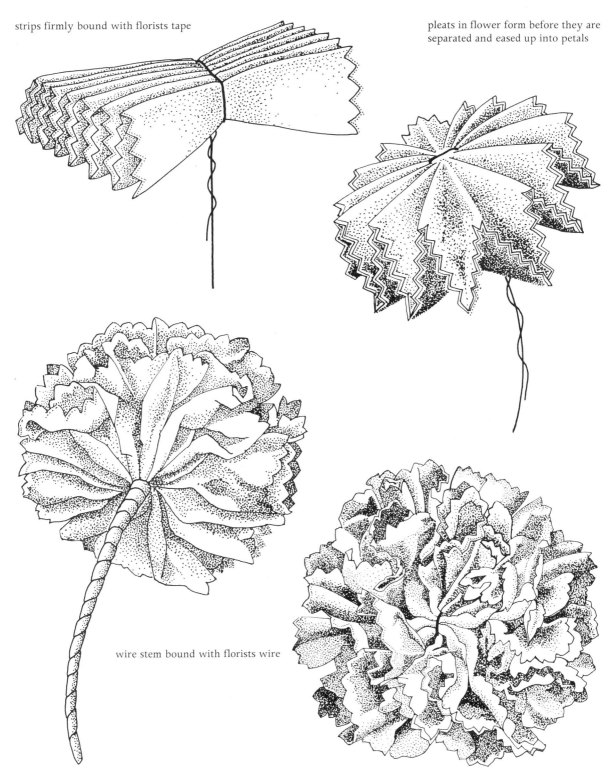

strips firmly bound with florists tape

pleats in flower form before they are separated and eased up into petals

wire stem bound with florists wire

finished flower

Flowers and leaves from foil

Material required: Sheets of kitchen foil or foil paper; stub wire
24 gauge (0·56mm); glue

Cut the paper into strips; each strip must be double the size of
the petal as it is now folded over and cut double. Cut several strips
in varying sizes. Place stub wires all along this strip at intervals
inside. Then glue the sides together. When dry, cut between each
wire so that little oblongs are left. Now fold the oblong in half,
lengthwise, before cutting it into a leaf shape. To make a leaf,
simply cover the wire with tape; but to make a flower, group at
least five of these shapes together with a centre to make a stamen.
A bead or small seed-head can be used for this. The flowers can be
in several layers if preferred, starting with the small shapes inside
and using larger ones for the outer layer.

There are other methods of cutting foil flowers but I find this
one very straight-forward and, because of the wire centre, easy
to bend into pretty shapes. All kinds of colour combinations suggest themselves – gold with silver, silver with blue. The secret
with these kinds of decorations is to make them as showy as
possible and not to attempt realism.

Roses

Material required: Crepe paper; stub wires 24 gauge (0·56mm);
florist's tape; reel or fuse wire

Cut across the roll of crepe paper, cutting a strip about 2-in
(5cm) wide – this is for the centres. Now cut another strip about
3-in (8cm) and a third 4-in (9cm). Cut the petals from these two
strips but be sure that the paper is cut across the bias – it means
that it is possible to pull *across* the petals, not lengthwise. The petals
can be cut in several layers all at once, to keep them uniform and to
save time. Each flower requires about five small and seven large
petals. When they are cut, stretch them gently between your thumb
and fingers so that they bulge slightly in the middle.

Now start by taking a piece of the 2-in strip about 4-in (9cm)
long. Place the stub wire on this, fold the paper down and make a
sort of little roll, to look like the tight centre of a rose. Holding this
in one hand, start to place the petals around, commencing with the
small ones and binding them on with reel wire. It is possible to vary
the shape of the rose by making some flowers with the petals facing
outwards for a full-blown look, or facing them inwards for a tighter
bloom. Obviously the size of the finished flower can be varied by
using small or large petals and by the number of layers. Bind the
finished stem with florist's tape or strips of green crepe paper.

These roses can be made to look very realistic by making them
in natural rose colours, or frankly artificial and exotic by using
black, brown or something rather outrageous. They could also be
tipped with silver or gold by putting a small amount of colourless
glue at the edge of the petal before dipping it into glitter.

I have also waxed them very successfully. To do this, I melt down any spare candles; if there happens to be a candle in the same colour as the paper, use that, but white will do quite well. Melt the wax in an old saucepan, take it outside the house (otherwise it can make an awful mess). Take with you a large tin or tall jar to stand the roses in while they are cooling. Just dip the finished rose quickly in the wax, shake off the surplus and leave to dry. This takes only a matter of seconds so be sure the flower shape is exactly as finally required before it is waxed. It is impossible to alter it afterwards.

Crepe paper roses (white ones are also waxed)

Pot trees

Material required: Dried or plastic flowers, seed-heads, fruits, cones, etc. (not pointed shapes but fairly thick and rounded). Ribbon; baubles; yoghurt or cream pot; thin stick about 9-in (23cm) long; plaster mixture; paint; glitter; stub wires 24 gauge (0·56mm); old pieces of oasis formed into a ball and wrapped in foil; or a ball of dried foam about the size of a tennis ball

Mount all the dried material on short pieces of stub wire about 2in (5cm) long. Weight the pot with small stones, then fill it with a fairly firm plaster mixture. Insert the stick in the centre and allow to set. Then wind a piece of string or a rubber band near the top before impaling the foam ball (this is to prevent it slipping down).

Cover the ball with flower heads, leaving space for the baubles and bows (but don't put these in until later). This takes quite a lot of material. Now spray the heads, stick and pot, and sprinkle some glitter on the flower or seed-heads. When this is dry, fill in with the bows and baubles and finish off with a matching streamer just underneath the ball.

This can be done with fresh material but in this case use oasis well soaked then wrapped in foil. Cupresses or holly look good with scarlet waterproof ribbon and baubles. The whole thing can be increased in scale, using a broom-stick in a large tub, to stand outside a front door or in a church porch.

And, of course, it can be adapted for summer flowers. With a basis of fresh foliage such as Box, it looks lovely with carnations or chrysanthemums for parties or weddings.

Water lily candle-holders

Material required: Sheets of gold or silver foil paper; stub wires 24 gauge (0·56mm); cardboard; glue; plasticine; tinsel; candle

Cut a strip of foil about 8-in (19cm) wide. Fold this over length-wise. Place short lengths of stub wire, just slightly longer than the folded width, all along this strip at about 3-in (8cm) intervals. Glue the sides of the strip together and allow to dry. Then cut between each wire so that there is a little oblong. Fold this in half, lengthwise, and cut to make a leaf shape. Now repeat all this with a slightly narrower strip. One lily takes about nine large leaves, eight smaller and another eight smaller still.

Cut a circle of strong cardboard about 4-in (10cm) in diameter. Shape the leaves gently (the wires allow this to be done) so that they are slightly curved. Then, starting from the outside with the largest leaves, glue them around the circle in three layers, leaving a space for the candle in the centre; the candle is anchored with plasticine or oasis fix. A strip of tinsel around the base of the candle, or a sprinkling of glitter, disguises this. If the candle is not to be lit, dip the wick in glue and glitter, too. This candle-holder looks very pretty made in layers of gold and silver.

Plastic trees

Material required: Two sprays of white plastic leaves or fern from a chain store. Try to find one with about seven branches on each spray. Stub wires 22 gauge (0·71mm); tape or crepe paper; yoghurt or cream pot; plaster mixture; paint and glitter

Pull all the branches off the two main stems (they come off quite easily) and give each one a false stem with a stub wire. Cover this with florist's tape or crepe paper strips. Now put all the stems together in a shape as near that of a tree as possible. Start with one stem in the hand, then place the next stem about one-inch lower and bind them together. Use tape or crepe-strips to do this and continue downwards at one-inch intervals until all the stems have been used. Then cut the wires neatly at the bottom, leaving enough to go into the pot. Bend the main stem to look rather like a Japanese Bonsai tree with some nice curves.

Silver and gold trees made from plastic fern

Now put a few small stones into the pot, for weight, before filling it with the plaster mixture. Insert the stem of the little tree into this, but do be careful to get it in the centre because it will be too late when it is dry. Try to support it as it sets so that it doesn't move. Make the mixture fairly thick so that it will set quite quickly.

When it is firm, spray the whole thing with silver, gold or copper and sprinkle some glitter over the leaves. I find that the pot needs at least two coats of paint. These little trees look extremely pretty without any further decoration, but they could be trimmed with tiny crackers, miniature baubles or bows.

Hanging arrangments
Using Metal Coat-hangers
Material required: Cheap metal coat-hangers; wadding; reel wire; ribbon; strips of foil or crepe paper; tinsel; baubles; dried flowers or seed-heads

Pull the coat-hanger into a ring or diamond shape, leaving the hook intact. Pad the wire with wadding, then cover this with ribbon, strips of foil or crepe paper, securing it firmly at each end with reel wire. There is a wide choice then for items to be wired on to the circle, either all the way round or just at the top or the base. Cones, seed-heads, dried flower heads, etc, can be painted and glittered and ribbon streamers and baubles added. Or cover the ring first with crepe paper then wire on clusters of waterproof ribbon all the way round. Bind the ribbon into loops, using a fairly wide ribbon, then tear each loop into strips. This ribbon splits very easily. If the clusters are bound closely together in contrasting colours, it looks very effective.

The hangers can also be used to make a ring of fresh evergreens. Prepare a number of small clusters of laurel, cupresses, holly, ivy, etc, and wire these closely together all the way round, placing each bunch to cover the stems of the previous one. Finish off with a large scarlet bow of waterproof ribbon. This will last a long time; if it is made some time ahead of Christmas, keep it in a cool place and give it an occasional spray of water.

A kissing ring can be made by using two hangers, one inside the other.

Birdcage
Buy a round or oval frame meant for a lampshade and cover the struts. A glittery one looks rather glamorous, so silver tinsel could be wound around the struts. Hang some silver or gold baubles inside the cage and perch a little glittery bird on the top.

If this is to be done with fresh material, cover the struts with scarlet ribbon, wrap some soaked oasis in foil and wire it to the inside of the cage. Stick evergreens into this and some trailing sprays of ivy to come down and outside the wire. Glue and glitter the edges of the ivy, add a few red bows and perch an artificial robin on the top.

A hanging decoration for
Christmas, made on a
lampshade frame

If a wicker plantpot holder is available, turn the plants out for a few days and fill the holder with evergreens. Put in some well-soaked oasis, either in a small dish or wired to the holder (covered in foil, of course) and insert evergreens.

Mobiles

Material required: Paper plates; paint and glitter; gold or silver thread or tinsel; baubles

Spray the paper plates on both sides and sprinkle with glitter. Even add a few stick-on stars. Now, starting from the outside, cut the plate into spirals about 1-in (2cm) wide – rather like peeling an apple in one piece. Attach the top of the spiral to the ceiling, then thread a bauble on a long piece of tinsel or silver thread and hang this through the centre.

Make a fairly even round ball of mesh wire, then give it an extra spray of silver paint. Spike it all over with silvered and glittered twigs, stiff tinsel strips or anything similar so that it looks like a glittery hedgehog. Suspend it from the centre or in a corner of the room.

Cover some long stub wires with tinsel, bend them in the centre and wire them together before suspending on a long piece of thread.

Door decorations

Proceed in a similar way to that described in the section on hanging arrangements, using metal coat-hangers. Alternatively, metal wreath rings, or rings of dry foam, can be bought from the florist.

As a change from the conventional material, use browns, yellows and orange; the brown provided by dried seed-heads, cones – in fact any kind of rounded dried material. Add nuts; the texture of walnuts looks very attractive, and they are easy to attach if a piece of thin reel wire is bound firmly round between the two halves. Clusters of beech masts, honesty in small groups and some plastic hellebores (Christmas roses) can be added. Also clusters of the small brightly coloured plastic fruit which is widely available in shops around Christmas. This is fairly expensive, but it can be washed after use and stored for another year.

Wire all the material to the ring and finish it off with a large bow of waterproof ribbon, picking up one of the colours in the material.

A cheap and easy foundation for a door decoration is a large potato wrapped in foil. Push a skewer right through and then put a cord or wire through the hole for hanging before stabbing holes with the skewer all over the potato and inserting holly or any kind of evergreen. The potato will keep the foliage fresh for some time. Add a bow of waterproof ribbon and, if the holly is bare, some artificial holly berries. A similar effect can be obtained by wrapping a block of soaked oasis in foil.

If there is any doubt about the safety of door decorations during the night, just suspend them by a long strong wire right over the

Plate 1
A Christmas pedestal using
fresh foliage and scarlet paper
carnations. FRANCIS WELLS

top of the door frame, anchored from inside. At night, simply lift the decoration and transfer it to the inside of the door.

Swags

Swags can be made with rolled mesh wire; in my book on drying and preserving flowers I have given details for many of these. Other methods include using a long plastic fern leaf, which can be sprayed gold or silver before wiring cones, baubles and similar items down the centre.

Alternatively use a plastic sink mat in white or red. Fix a Christmassy arrangement to the centre with foam or plasticine. If it is a square mat, hang it from one of the corners. A dried swag can be sprayed gold – silver looks just a little cold for a swag. Any kind of dried and plastic material can be combined very successfully.

Christmas swag of silver and gold

Plate 2
An Easter bonnet

Crackers

Material required: Cardboard cylinders from kitchen rolls or toilet
    paper; paper to cover – crepe or anything pretty; sticky tape;
    decoration

Home-made crackers can be made to look really glamorous,
although, of course, they will not 'pull'. However, they can hold a
small gift, and it is possible to make them to harmonize with
whatever colour scheme has been chosen for the table. Mats and
napkin rings can also be made to match.

First of all, tuck the gift inside the cardboard cylinder. Cut the
paper so that it goes well around the cylinder and overlaps at the
back and at both ends. Usually this is about 7-in (18cm) around with
a 4-in (10cm) overlap at each end. Fix the paper at the back with
sticky tape and press the cracker down very slightly so that it does
not roll about when finished. Now push the paper in at each end
and where it meets the cylinder. If it is creased very firmly, it will
stay put without any other aid. Attach a piece of plasticine to the
front and insert the decoration. Make a pretty and well-designed
miniature arrangement with tiny dried or plastic flowers and leaves,
painted and glittered – ribbon roses, seed-heads, small baubles or
beads. If the crackers are for children, the floral arrangement could
be replaced by glued-on cut-out figures.

*Crackers made from cardboard
cylinders, covered with crepe
paper and decorated with dried
flowers, foil leaves or stick-on
stars*

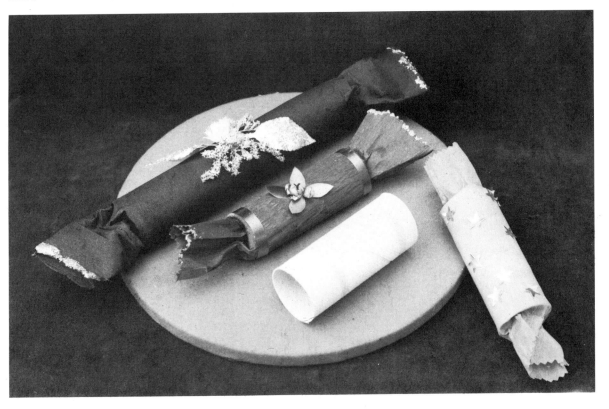

Decorated parcels
LEFT *wrapped in white tissue,
red silver-edged ribbon, silver
foil leaves, red ribbon roses*
RIGHT *wrapped with kitchen
foil, foil leaves and baubles*
FRONT *Crinkle foil wrapping,
ribb on sprinkled with glue and
glitter, foil leaves and flowers*

Decorated parcels

Cover any kind of box with suitable paper and match it with ribbon and a decoration of glittered and painted flowers instead of a bow; these can be dried or plastic. I have done one in dull silver wrapping paper with pale blue ribbon and blue and silver flowers; and with tiny leaves made from the same wrapping paper.

First, don't get carried away with the decoration and forget to put the gift inside the box right at the start! Then wrap the parcel *very* neatly and attach the ribbon with sticky tape. Fix a small lump of oasis fix or plasticine at the join on the ribbons to take the flowers. Another and rather cheaper way with paper is to use ordinary white tissue and tie it with ribbon (scarlet looks particularly attractive at Christmas); and to make little ribbon roses for the decoration.

To make ribbon roses, use silk or satin ribbon – waterproof ribbon is too stiff for these. Take a length, according to the size of the rose required, and roll the first inch (2cm) into a tight roll. Then, holding the roll firmly in one hand, continue to roll the ribbon lightly around it, twisting as you go. Be careful not to let the centre roll go or the whole thing will fall apart and you will have to start all over again. When the length of ribbon is used, bind it tightly together with reel wire. These roses seem very difficult at first, but once the knack is acquired by practice, it becomes easy. Matching leaves can be made by doubling the ribbon over and sticking it together after inserting a small short piece of wire. Then cut out a leaf shape and neaten the edges by glueing lightly before dipping into glitter.

Bottles are always difficult to wrap, but a useful container is a long carton which has held sponge-cakes. Cover this first with pretty paper. If the bottle is too awkward for any kind of carton, do not attempt to wrap it but attach a small glittered arrangement to the neck with plasticine. Cereal cartons can be used, too, for other awkwardly shaped gifts. It is possible to make your own bags. Take two rectangular pieces of wrapping paper and place them at right angles to each other. Now fold over a 'hem' on three sides – right, left and bottom – and glue this in place, leaving a flap at the top. These bags can be dressed up in all kinds of ways. If they are made in plain silver, gold or coloured paper a message, or the name of the recipient, can be written in glue and then glittered.

The Christmas cake

Use one of the little white pedestals which are designed for a tiered wedding cake and attach a silvered and glittered decoration of flowers and tiny baubles to the top of this with plasticine. Cut a length of wide white ribbon long enough to go round the outside of the cake; dip the edge of the ribbon into colour-less glue and then in silver glitter. Pin this to the cake and attach a small arrangement, in plasticine, to complement the cake pedestal on the top.

Table decorations

The golden rule for table decorations, apart from buffets, is to be able to see across them, but this does not necessarily mean that they must always be low. Something quite delicate will leave enough vision; another way of obtaining height without sacrificing conversation, is to put tall candles in a low arrangement.

A variation of this is to use beautiful candlesticks and to place the flowers in a ring around the base. They will be in foam, of course, and if this is wet, the table must be well protected. A ring of foam rubber and some doubled foil is usually sufficient, but I do suggest trying out its capabilities beforehand. The party could be ruined for the hostess if she has to sit and watch a lovely table getting spoiled.

I suppose on the whole it might be better to use either dried and glittered material at Christmas (this is a great time saver) or foliage (a *money* saver). The plastic trees described on page 40 could be used – a large one as a centre-piece and a small one at each place. Or small shells, painted silver or gold with a glittered arrangement, one at each place.

A low centre-piece with ribbon streamers radiating to each place setting looks most attractive, especially on a round table. Use wide ribbon to tone with the colour of the arrangement and add a small posy or corsage, with perhaps a decorated matchbox for the men. A good idea, if there is time to carry it out, would be to make small parcels as described earlier, but all in colours to match the table design.

Nothing looks more festive at Christmas than a plain white cloth with a centre arrangement of foliage, red berries and a very few white flowers, or even plastic hellebores (Christmas roses). Some tall red candles in the centre (see the section on More Ideas for inserting candles) and broad scarlet ribbons to each place is very effective. If it is a buffet table, loop the ribbons along the front and catch the loops with small arrangements of matching flowers and foliage.

Cones or Pyramids

I have described in my book on drying flowers how to make wire cones, so I simply add some suggestions for filling them.

A very gay and unusual one can be made with tiny plastic fruits, available at most large stores, in shades of yellow, orange and green. Add small gold dried flowers and seed-heads (it is better not to glitter for this design) tiny baubles and gilded cones. If a pair of candlesticks is available, make two matching rings, either in foam or mesh wire netting. Fill them with matching material and place them around the base of the candlesticks. I put my cone, with a candlestick on either side, on a long narrow board covered in a muted green velvet; in this way the design is integrated and can be easily moved when necessary.

Fruit Pyramid

I saw this in the United States, in Colonial Williamsburg in fact, where the old traditional style of arrangements are still done, especially in dried flowers and at Christmas.

The foundation is made, as far as I could see, from a rounded block of wood, about 3-in (7cm) in diameter and 12-in (30cm) high with a flattened top fixed to a firm base. Butchers' skewers or long thin-headed nails were put into the block at staggered intervals (holes would need to be drilled for these) with the nails or skewers shorter towards the top. The bottom layer must not be too near the base of the block, otherwise there would not be enough room for the fruit.

Choose good coloured apples and oranges, not too large and using the largest at the base, graduating the size towards the top. Impale them in even rows onto the nails – either a row of each fruit, or apples and oranges alternately. Place a pineapple on the flat top and fill in the spaces between the fruit with sprigs of evergreen or nuts.

Napkin rings and table mats

Material required: Cardboard cylinders from kitchen towels or
   toilet paper; ordinary cardboard, neither too thick or too thin,
   but pliable; paper to cover; glue; decorations

Cut across the cylinder, very neatly, in rings about $1\frac{1}{2}$-in (3cm) wide and cover these with the chosen paper. Attach a decoration with plasticine. A very simple decoration is just a strip of tinsel around the middle of the ring – but it can be as simple or as elaborate as you like.

The table mats look rather pretty if they are cut in a star shape and covered with paper. I have used gold and silver alternately for this idea, with a gold decoration on the silver and *vice versa*. Just strips of tinsel attached to the edge to match the rings is quick and easy; or it could be some flat pressed flowers stuck over the surface of the mat, with a matching design on paper napkins.

Mantelpieces

A wide mantelpiece can be given an unusual look with hanging arrangements at the side instead of along the top. For this it is necessary to use two narrow pieces of wood, one for each side, the length dictated by the height from the ground. Fix long pieces of foam to the boards, well-soaked and wrapped in foil if it is for fresh material. Attach one piece at the top and another about two-thirds of the way down the board; this makes it possible to get a lovely flowing effect with either fresh or dried material. The arrangement can be kept quite light and delicate; at Christmas I use glittered and painted material when the fire is alight. Fresh flowers and foliage do not last very long in these circumstances, but look attractive for a summer party or wedding. I use glittered ferns, statice, strands of pampas grass and skeleton hydrangea and magnolia.

For a top decoration, anchor a bare branch firmly at one end of the mantelpiece. A very strong pinholder will usually be all right, but for added safety invert another pinholder on top of this, just catching the pins at the side. The branch could be given a light covering of artificial frost before use. Cover the remainder of the shelf with cotton wool (anchored very firmly because of fire hazards) and then sprinkle with frost. Hang baubles from the branch – they will move gently in the heat from the fire. Add a few reindeer or a tiny Father Christmas with a sleigh, or some of the figures which the children have made.

Finally, be sure to look at all mantelpiece arrangements while you are sitting down!

Junior Christmas

It is good to try to involve the children with the Christmas preparations, other than just decorating the tree. So I have included some fairly simple things which most children could attempt.

Bells from egg cartons
Material required: Opaque egg boxes; glue; glitter; ribbon or tinsel

Cut around each egg shape to make a little bell. Touch the edges with colourless glue, then dip it in glitter. Thread a ribbon or tinsel through the top, knot it inside and group several together at different lengths to make a cluster of bells.

Figures
Father Christmas or Angels.
Material required: Thin cardboard; silver or gold paper doilies (for angels); white or red crepe paper (for Father Christmas); ball of dried foam or tissue paper

Cut the thin cardboard then fold it into a cone. Glue the ball of foam to the top or crumple the tissue paper into a ball – even a table tennis ball will do.

For Father Christmas, cut a cloak and hood from red crepe paper and stick some cotton wool on the ball to make a nice beard and some side whiskers. The ball can be painted, but it doesn't really have to be a proper face.

If it is to be an angel, cut a cloak of white crepe paper and cover this with a gold or silver doiley. Glue some artificial 'Angel's hair' on the ball (or strands of wool will do) and make a little halo from some strips of doiley. Make wings from the doiley, too, but fold these in half so that they have two good sides; also it gives extra strength.

Stars
Material required: Drinking straws; cotton; glue and glitter

Place two straws in the form of a cross, then build up in between to make star shapes, binding each straw very firmly with strong cotton in the centre. Brush with colourless glue, then glitter. Make several of these and string them up at irregular intervals to make a mobile.

How to make angels from drinking straws

Straw Angels

Material required: 17 straws (stalks of corn will do, if cut level); thread; pipe cleaner; cotton wool or pingpong ball or bauble; wool; cotton wool or angel's hair (for hair)

Take seven of the straws and cut them to about 3-in (7cm). Bind the thread tightly around the exact middle, so that the straws go into a fan shape. This is for the wings. Take the other ten straws and cut to double the length of the first group. Now tie the thread tightly around this bundle, again in the middle; these will also fan out. Bend them over in the middle, then stick the ball (or whatever is to make the head) to the pipe cleaner. Push the pipe cleaner through the top of the long bunch of straws and secure it firmly. Push the wings underneath one of the straws at the back and either stick it or tie firmly. Now tie another thread tightly around the main bundle to make a waist. Bend two of the straws at the sides to make arms (cut them shorter to do this). Add hair to the head and paint a face if desired. These angels can, of course, be made larger or smaller if required.

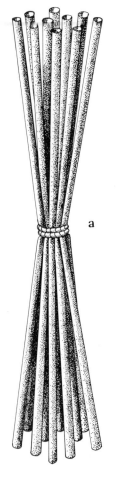

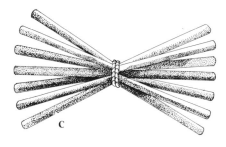

a and b Bundle of straws tightly tied in the middle then bent to form body

c Wings

d Pipe cleaner pushed through small hole in pingpong ball

e Pipe cleaner loop pushed into bauble

f finished angel

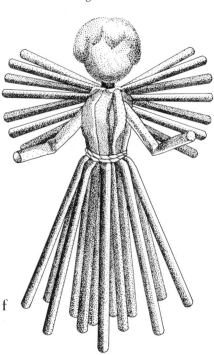

Calendars

Material required: Cardboard, fairly strong but soft enough to cut, any colour; dried or pressed flowers; glue; ribbon; brown paper; small hanging calendars to attach; for pressed flowers – very thin transparent plastic film

Cut the cardboard very neatly, about 3-in (8cm) by 9-in (23cm), and a piece of brown paper slightly smaller.

There are now two different methods, according to whether dried or pressed flowers are being used.

Dried flowers: Cut a piece of ribbon for the hanging loop, about 6-in (15cm) long and glue this firmly to the back of the cardboard at the top centre. Cut two more pieces, each about 3-in (8cm) long and glue these in the centre bottom, a little apart, to take the hanging calendar. Glue the calendar on to the ribbon strips and neaten this at the back with sticky tape. Now turn the calendar to the back and glue on the brown paper to hide the ribbon ends and to neaten the back. Turn the calendar back and start to glue on a pretty design of dried flowers. Helichrysum heads and other dried flowers which can be bought at most florists look nice if you have no dried material of your own.

For pressed flowers proceed as follows: cut the cardboard, brown paper and also the ribbon as above, but design and attach the pressed flowers to the front of the calendar first. Cover this with very thin plastic, taking it over to the back very neatly. The self-sealing type is easiest to use. Then attach the ribbon loop to the calendar and finally neaten off the back with the brown paper.

A decoration for the mantelpiece

About 24 small plastic bells or the same amount of papier mache seed pots. If seed pots are used, spray them with gold or silver-paint and add some glitter. String the bells on a long piece of cord or a strip of tinsel and attach to each end of the mantelpiece (not while the fire is alight!). Loop up the middle with a large bow or ribbon or a piece of sticky tape.

A roll of kitchen foil can be used to make a Christmas message. Pencil the words on the foil very lightly, then cut around them. It is possible to cut out 'Merry Christmas' or something similar in one long strip if you are careful to leave a small link between each letter. Otherwise, single letters can be cut and attached to coloured ribbon or tape.

Collect the empty date boxes and either cover them in small pieces of fabric, silver or gold paper, or spray them with paint. Anchor a short candle in the centre with plasticine, then fill up with pebbles or stones to weight the box safely. Hide these with sprigs of evergreen or baubles.

The crackers, napkin rings and place-mats described earlier are also suitable for older children to make.

Shells

Collect sea shells during the summer. Fill them with a small piece of plasticine and make little arrangements of dried flowers, or plastic, in them. Spray the whole thing with gold or silver paint, then sprinkle on some glitter.

Gift tags

Material required: Small dried flower heads, painted and glittered; cardboard (white or coloured); glue; glitter; pinking shears; ribbon

Cut the cardboard into a square or rectangle with the pinking shears. Make a neat hole in one corner and thread the ribbon through this. Tie it in a knot but leave enough room to attach it to a parcel. Glue a flower head on one corner, then glue the edges of the cardboard before dipping them in glitter.

A variation is to buy a packet of gold or silver stars from the stationer and stick these on the cardboard. The stars can also be stuck around a candle to make it look Christmassy.

Nativity crib

Make a cardboard crib by folding a piece of cardboard about 3-in (8cm) wide and 18-in (54cm) long for the roof. Bend this in the middle, then cut a matching triangle to fit in the back space and stick this on with sticky tape. Now cover the roof with straw to look like thatch. Sometimes this can be got from wine-merchants or from a farm. If it is not possible to find thatch, use cheap white cotton wool to resemble snow, or take some pine cones to pieces and stick the scales on to look like roof tiles.

Christmas cards

Material required: Thin coardboard; glue; 'flower' braid

Cut a small card to whatever size is required. Remember it has to be folded over and cut around the edge with pinking shears. It need not necessarily be square or oblong – a semicircle or a full circle looks pretty, too. Then cut another piece just slightly smaller to go inside; this could even be in a different colour. Glue the small piece lightly down the centre fold and insert it in the cover. The message can be written on this inside piece. Now fold the card in two and begin to decorate the front. Cut out each tiny flower from the braid and glue them in a pattern around the edges. Add a small pressed leaf to each flower if wanted; fill in the centre of the card cover with cut-outs from other old cards. This idea can be adapted for use as birthday or Mother's Day cards.

Engagements and Weddings

Engagements

Two hearts

There are various ways of making hearts for flower arranging. One of the easiest is to use cheap metal coat-hangers and bend them into the right shape. Make two of these (remove the hooks unless it is to be a hanging arrangement) and bind the wire with wadding or cotton wool or foam rubber – anything to pad them out a bit. Cover this with ribbon or foil, and wire on a well-soaked piece of foam wrapped in foil at the base of each heart. Do a pastel arrangement in one and something more vivid in the other. Make an arrow from a piece of cane, wrap this in foil and link the two hearts together with the arrow.

The heart theme can be carried further by adding cut-out hearts to the tablecloth here and there.

A ring centre-piece

Cover a shallow square box – any kind of box – with a piece of black velvet. Wrap some soaked foam in a long strip of foil and shape it round into a ring. Now stud it closely with yellow-gold flowers for the main part and another suitable jewel colour to look like a gem in the centre. This can be made into a double arrangement by doing one ring with a jewel in the centre and another plain gold.

Other ideas

There is a varied assortment of containers with a cherub or cupid base and these are really very pretty for this occasion. They are usually more suitable for buffet parties because they face one way but they can be made to look rather special by the addition of ribbon streamers in the flower colours.

An arrangement on the top of a champagne bottle looks very festive. Special holders are made to fit into bottles. The main arrangement could be surrounded by smaller ones in champagne glasses. Line the glasses with foil before putting in the foam as this disguises the rather prominent green. Small silver or gold doilies look pretty inside glasses too.

Pink, green and white would be an attractive colour scheme for this party. With pink champagne maybe, or a rosé wine, pink smoked salmon, pink paté (anything can be coloured by the addition of harmless vegetable colouring), green salads, cucumber mousse, strawberries and raspberries, etc. Use candles – and of course china – in the same colours, too.

A heart for an engagement
party, made from foam,
covered with fabric and pleated
ribbon edge, glued on.
Arrangement of pastel
coloured flowers, in foil wrapped
foam

For a winter party, when flowers were scarce and expensive, I
made a group of feather flowers (described on page 82) in very
pale pink with a touch of delicate green feather foliage. They were
not only economical but a very good talking point!

If a little china hand can be found, it is fun to decorate the
engagement finger with a little ring of flowers and to repeat this
on a larger scale around the base of the hand. Put foil underneath
first.

Weddings
The church
The first thing about decorating a church for any occasion is to
make sure that the bride has consulted the clergy in charge and
that there are no objections. Sometimes it is felt that there should
not be flowers on the altar, and it is wise to get this quite clear before
a scheme is decided upon. It is also sensible to make sure that there
is no other wedding before or after. I well remember stripping
down what we thought were finished arrangements (but in sur-
prisingly good condition!) only to find that they had been done for
the ceremony which was to precede our particular one. If there is
another bride on the same day, it is sometimes possible to combine
and to share the expense of flowers in the church.

Now go round the church with the bride and her mother and ask

56

where they would like to have the flowers. Perhaps they have no idea and will leave it entirely in the hands of the arranger, but they may have strong views, about colour for instance. So, however it may offend the taste of the arranger, remember it is the bride's day and her choice. Try to steer her away from too much blue, though, because it does disappear at a distance in most churches; suggest to her that the colours should harmonise with the dresses of the wedding party. Bridesmaids in pretty pink frocks really do not look very good surrounded by orange and yellow flowers. Try to follow one scheme of colour throughout.

Remember that as many arrangements as possible should be about shoulder height so that they can be seen by the congregation; and leave enough room by the sanctuary steps to allow four people to stand in comfort.

Many churches have sloping window sills, and a long thin slat of wood can be jammed at either end of the sill without using nails or any other support. A block of damp foil, wrapped foam or moss will rest on this. Or the same block can be secured by winding a long piece of reel wire around it and attaching this with sticky tape or drawing pins to the bottom edge of the window above.

One exception to the shoulder-high rule is arrangements on the pew ends. These look extremely pretty and are not difficult to do. Soaked foam again, in foil. There is usually a ledge or scroll which

Pot 'trees' outside a church porch for a wedding.
MARJORIE HARRIS AND PAT CRAWFORD

will serve to fix a string or wire, but remember to make the arrangement rather higher than wide so that it does not extend beyond the width of the pew side. If some of the pews have a stave, an arrangement can be suspended from this, too.

But let us return to the beginning, with a welcome in the church porch. Outside, pot trees are ideal for this but they must be large, preferably a broomstick in a tub or a very large flower pot. Place one on either side of the door. If the porch is suitable, it may also be possible to suspend an arrangement over the centre – perhaps a star, a bell or a cross of flowers. This is made with a foundation of mesh wire formed into the desired shape and filled with damp foam or moss. These can be made a few days in advance and will keep fresh if sprayed frequently.

A country church will probably have a porch seat, and nothing looks nicer here than simple baskets of garden flowers. If there are buttonholes for guests and ushers, these can be arranged in a basket here, too, with the addition of a ribbon bow perhaps.

Next, to the font; it can be decorated without restriction on this occasion. If it is opposite the main entrance door, so much the better; otherwise, try to place a pedestal here which catches the eye as one enters. Then, up the aisle to the chancel steps. Slightly lower pedestal arrangements here so as not to mask the large pedestals which are probably on either side of the altar. Asymmetrical arrangements, sloping towards each other, make a change here from the conventional triangle. Don't forget a small arrangement for the table where the register is to be signed; and, even if side chapels are not used, their emptiness can be disguised with very large arrangements.

I have learned by experience to avoid some of the snags which occur in decorating churches and it might be helpful to pass on a few ideas. The most obvious one is mentioned at the beginning of this chapter – to obtain the consent of the religious authorities.

But don't forget the ladies who regularly do the flowers; they work very hard at this during the year and may be inclined to resent strangers taking over. If the church has its own containers, seek permission to borrow these and try to use only foam and wire in them. There is then no need to return to retrieve precious pin-holders, but keep a list of anything used, such as tubes for pedestals. Don't go back too quickly to collect these, but allow the flowers to live out their lives giving pleasure to the church users, though of course the pew arrangements should not be left in place. If you have done a great many arrangements, it might be a good idea to offer to return later in the week to dismantle them and clear up. I always take plenty of newspaper, a brush and dustpan and a cloth. I allocate my flowers to each place on newspaper with a central pool of foliage in the porch, and I prepare the containers in advance. If I do the flowers before the wedding I try to return on the

An asymmetrical pedestal for a wedding, using lilies and carnations

day itself to spray each arrangement or to make plans for someone on the spot to do this.

When it is all finished and cleared up, go outside and come back to look around with a fresh eye. If you are returning to top up, leave a bucket with spare flowers and foliage tucked away in the vestry so that any faded material can be replaced next day.

Marquees

To be faced with decorating a marquee for the first time can be a daunting experience, and it is certainly a job for more than one person. Plan well ahead and remember that, ten to one, everything will be altered on the day anyway! Don't be thrown by this; if the plans are flexible, just change the positioning around and all will be well. Try to discover when the caterers will be there and to do the flowers, if possible, *after* they have set up the tables. Large men with large trestle tables are apt not to notice a basket of lilies beneath their feet!

If the marquee is striped, the colours must be taken into consideration, but in any case it is not a good idea to use dead-white flowers against a marquee wall – which is always very much off-white.

Decorations most suitable for marquee walls are garlands, swags or anything which can be attached firmly and will not be damaged if the wind is strong. The walls of a marquee can sway alarmingly and any ground-based arrangements can be in trouble. Flat baskets, such as bicycle baskets or flat-sided hanging baskets, can be filled and hung against the wall. Allow the plant material to flow down and over the sides and site the baskets well above the heads of the guests so that they are seen when the place is full.

Sometimes the supporting poles are covered with fabric and need no disguise, but often they are left bare and then they provide a good place for garlands. These can be made of fresh foliage, box, laurel, yew, etc. Roll pieces of newspaper into long lengths and attach the bunches of greenery with reel wire. If it is well-conditioned beforehand, it will last the length of a reception without water, but it could be surface-sprayed if necessary.

Plants can be grouped, in layers, at the base of the poles but it is risky to use many pedestals in marquees – the ground is usually uneven and the crush of people can hide them anyway. Perhaps just one lovely one behind the bride. But if any other form of decoration is needed, pot trees are better. Wedge a broom handle in a large tub, well-weighted with stones. Wire a large ball of moss, covered with mesh wire, to the top and insert flowers and foliage into this. A ribbon streamer underneath the ball of flowers can pick up the colours. It is possible to make these trees well beforehand with lots of foliage and insert just a few rather large flowers – carnations, chrysanthemums – at the last minute.

If pot trees are used, it is a nice idea to repeat them on the buffet table. They don't take up much room and stand very securely. I have described in my book *Drying and Preserving Flowers* (Batsford) how to make these trees.

Flowers in the house

Even if all the celebrations are elsewhere, don't entirely neglect the bride's home. Her mother will have neither time nor inclination to bother with flowers, but close friends are sure to be there at some time or another; and, anyway, when it's all over, how nice to have something lovely to look at!

If the reception is here, colours and position of arrangements are of course a matter of negotiation and personal taste. Obviously wall swags are not suitable, but still try to keep arrangements as high as possible.

A welcome at the door is nice, either with pot trees as described earlier, or with a door circle. This could be made on a wire coat-hanger with roses or anything available. The method is detailed in the chapter on Christmas. If there is an attractive fireplace, the bride and groom could stand in front of this and swags could be placed on either side – again as detailed under Christmas – but with fresh flowers.

If it is a large room, make an arch with some cheap trellis (if it is against a wall, back it with plastic or foil for protection) and insert lots of foliage and some flowers at the last moment. With these well-conditioned, they will last the length of the reception. A really tall pedestal could make a good background or alternatively two smaller ones on either side of the receiving group.

Many of the ideas described under Christmas and Parties can be adapted for a wedding by using fresh flowers.

Fun spoons

Add a traditional touch – and some fun – to a wedding or engagement party by using wooden spoons as part of the decoration.

To make these, first drill a small hole through the top of the handle so that ribbon can be threaded through and the spoons hung up. The design can be carried out in fresh or dried material; it is fixed to the place where the spoon handle meets the bowl, either with foam in foil or plasticine. I find that if I use colourful dried flowers, these are more satisfactory as they can be kept by guests or bridesmaids as souvenirs.

I dye natural dried material with Dylon dyes and, for a wedding, would follow the colours of the bridesmaids' dresses if possible. A small piece of plasticine is fixed very firmly (I make mine extra secure by winding sticky tape over and around it), then make a pretty shape with whatever material is being used, add ribbon in a matching shade, and hang them around the room or put them at place settings.

Decorated wooden spoons.
Dried flowers inserted in
plasticine; ribbon handles

A wedding cake decorated with
fresh flowers. Spray
chrysanthemums, Iceberg roses

Flowers for the cake

Avoid those horrid little silvered vases which the caterers so often supply for the top of a wedding cake and use instead either a small low wine glass or a tiny white container. Line a wine glass with foil, then a piece of soaked foam and arrange delicate flowers in an all-round triangle shape. A tiered cake can have matching decorations if a small piece of soaked foam is foil-wrapped and then attached to a ribbon surrounding the cake. Don't make the foam too wet and do the arrangement before attaching it to the cake, otherwise some water may leak and ruin the icing.

The cake table

Do use a round table for a round cake and a square one for a square cake. It sounds obvious but many people don't think about it until it is too late. Likewise for the cake stand; I really have seen a square cake on a round stand!

It is also a nice idea to try to pick up a little colour, perhaps the bridesmaids' dresses, by using a table cloth of some pastel shade first and then covering this with layers of net, nylon or tulle. Make small posies, matching the cake flowers – these can be in moss or foam but if well-conditioned and made not too early, they will last long enough without anything. Loop up the net with the posies, linking them with matching ribbon streamers.

Wedding Anniversaries

1st – Cotton

Cotton seems a very workaday substance for such an important anniversary so perhaps it is a good idea to inject a little fun into an arrangement for this occasion.

One simple idea is to impale various reels of cotton, in suitable colours, on knitting needles or strong stub wire and place these here and there in an arrangement of fresh flowers. The cotton can be used afterwards, so it is not too extravagant.

A more complicated suggestion is to make flowers of white or coloured cotton. Cut two leaf shapes, stitch these together leaving a small gap at the base. Turn the petal inside-out and insert a wire. Try to get this around the edge of the petal if the cotton isn't very stiff. Then put a slightly stronger wire in as a stem. Or use stiff lining fabric, which needs no stitching. Cut two petals, place a wire along the centre and iron the two together. Make as many of these as required, then group some together to make a flower, with a bead or a pearl in the centre for the stamen. Use single petals as leaves.

2nd – Paper

Paper flowers of any kind – and these are not as nasty as they may sound!

ROSES. To make crepe paper roses, cut petals from the crepe paper, making sure that they are cut across the bias, so that the paper can be stretched. Hold the petal between the thumb and finger of both hands and press gently with the thumb so that the petal bulges slightly, to give a rose petal shape. Roll a small piece of paper into a tight tube for the centre, then group the petals around and secure them with reel wire.

Make petals in varying sizes. The large roses take about twelve petals, decreasing in size as required. Mount each finished rose on a thick stub wire or false stem and bind this in green.

WATER LILIES. See under 'Christmas'.

CARNATIONS. See under 'Christmas'. Use the same method but in different colours. White, pale pink or pale yellow look very pretty with real foliage.

TISSUE PAPER FLOWERS. Use the paper folded over double and cut a petal shape but do not cut through at the base – so that, in effect, there is a piece shaped rather like a pair of spectacles. Make as many of these as the size of the flower requires. Place the stub wires across the centre fold, one by one, and push a group gently together. Cover the stub wire with tape or paper.

3rd – Leather

I cannot recommend making leather flowers, though I suppose it would be possible, if expensive. However, a good substitute could be some of the dried material, such as laurel, which dries with a very leather-like surface. For a contrast in textures, combine this with the matt surfaces which look like suede. If there is a nice piece of chamois leather available, use it as a base. It makes a good window or car cleaner afterwards!

4th – Fruit and Flowers

Very obvious, and no problem to the flower arranger. Combine grapes, apples impaled on cocktail sticks, tomatoes (they are fruit) – indeed anything which harmonises with the chosen flowers.

5th – Wooden

I think dried plant material makes the best interpretation for this, but it would also be possible to use fresh flowers in shades of cream through to coffee, on a wood base or in a wooden candlestick. Wood slices are sold for flower arranging or might be found at a sawmill. If these are bought in their natural state, do be sure to oil them first to prevent the wood splitting, and to store them flat. Combine the fresh flowers with a piece of contorted wood or driftwood. If there is no wood slice available, look around for a wood plate, a cheese or bread board. Lovely wood roses come from the cones of the cedar tree.

6th – Sugar

Fun again, and an arrangement not to be taken too seriously. Use white or sugar pink flowers and not too much foliage, and place some candy lollies among the flowers. Or make a feather or a plastic tree (see pages 40 and 80) and hang cube sugar from the branches.

7th – Woollen

Buy a ball or skein of wool in the colour of the chosen flowers, re-wind it into smaller balls and impale these on knitting needles here and there among the arrangement.

8th – Salt

The only thing I have been able to find that looks at all like salt is a block of white dry foam – the kind that is used for dried flowers. Stand it up (like Lot's wife!) and incorporate it into the arrangement or break it into small pieces and scatter among the flowers. Come to that, why *not* use a block of real household salt? Very useful if it is likely to snow.

9th – Copper

It is possible to buy sheets of thin copper and to make really lovely flowers which can be used all the year round and look most beautiful. Cut three circles, varying in size, then cut round the edge of each one in scallop shapes. Thread a firm stub wire through the centre of each with the smallest circle in the middle. Push each petal up gently from underneath into a rose shape, then cover the stub wires. Use with preserved beech leaves or some kind of foliage in similar shades.

If there is any kind of copper container around – a kettle, saucepan, jelly mould or colander – press this into service, and try to find apricot flowers to harmonize. There are roses, carnations, lilies, dahlias and chrysanthemums, for instance.

10th – Tin

Roses can be made in the same way as for copper, but use the sealer tops from inside tins for this, or kitchen foil wrong side out. Try to find some grey foliage, as too much green takes away the effect.

12th – Silk

Make roses as for the cotton anniversary, but this time with silk. Stand the finished arrangement on a piece of silk or a scarf, whichever is available. Try to use flowers with a silky texture, such as roses, tulips, etc.

15th – Crystal

Make some little crystal trees.

Material required: About 54 glass beads (varying sizes); silver reel wire; a small tin for the base (the top of an aerosol paint can is about the right size); plaster mixture

Each tree needs about nine branches, and I find it best to keep to beads of one colour; natural glass is best for this particular occasion.

Start the top branch with four beads, graduating the sizes. Thread the first bead on to a piece of wire about 10-in (25cm) long and doubled in half. Push the first bead to the top of this loop, then give the wire two or three twists under the bead to keep it in place. Proceed until the other three beads have been threaded, twisting between each one. Now make eight more branches, each one slightly longer than the last. Take all the branches and wire them together in a tree shape, starting of course with the smallest at the top and widening at the base. Wire them together with more reel wire and twist each branch so that it has pretty curves. Neaten the base and insert it into the small tin, which has been filled with plaster mixture. Prop it up while the plaster is drying so that it does not end up lop-sided; when dry, paint the plaster and the tin. One of these small trees could be made for each place setting and a larger one for the centre.

Another idea is to buy some large lumps of 'plastic' glass or to

Trees and flowers made with beads; a crystal 'tree' and pearl 'flowers' each suitable for relevant wedding anniversaries

use broken windscreen glass. Flower arrangers always push their broken windscreens outwards and collect the pieces! It is a very pretty green-ish glass and ideal to cover a pin-holder in a shallow dish.

I once used an old discarded chandelier as a centre-piece for a crystal anniversary. It was a very small one and made of plastic 'crystals'. So I turned it upside down and put a small tin in the centre, which I filled with white flowers.

20th – China

I suppose it is best to make a feature of the china when used for this occasion; but it is possible to make crepe paper flowers (as for the 2nd anniversary) and then to wax them so that they look like china.

This is easy – though messy – and can be done by melting down old candles. Use candles the colour of the paper if available, but white will do. Use an old saucepan and cover the cooker with news-paper. When the wax is liquid, dip the rose already made and mounted, very quickly into this. It is best to do it outdoors as the flower must be well-shaken immediately it is removed from the wax. They dry very quickly, so be sure the petals are arranged exactly as required before waxing since it is impossible to change them afterwards. These flowers can be washed, very gently, before putting them away for further use.

Plate 3
*A gold and silver glittered
arrangement for Christmas*

25th – Silver

Here is a chance to go to town on this very important anniversary. If there is any silver around which can be used as a container, make the best of whatever is available. Be sure to line silver items with polythene or foil so that they do not get scratched or damaged by wire or water. A tureen, a jug, a salver – anything can be adapted for use as a container, but do not despair if no silver is to hand. A tin of silver spray paint will transform even the shabbiest tin into an attractive container.

The flowers really should be white, with perhaps a discreet spray of artificially-made silver flowers, or some baubles, here and there. The cloth could be white and maybe the figures '25' cut from foil and glued on. If there is a white lace cloth around, spread this over a table covered with silver foil. Use white or silver candles, too; these can be bought with the figures 'twenty-five' already on them, but it is also an idea to cut more figures from foil and glue these to the candles as well. Make good use of silver doilies – for place mats or to use as bases for the flowers. Make the table glitter and look really glamorous.

30th – Pearl

Raid the bead box again, for pearls this time. Make little pearl flowers by stringing about ten to twelve pearls, graduating in size with largest in the centre, on to reel wire. Bend this round into a petal shape (see illustration). Take three to five of these for each flower, wire one large pearl on to a separate piece of wire for a centre, group the petals around and wire them all onto a strong stub wire. Cover the stem and mix the pearl flowers with fresh ones. If enough are made, the entire arrangement could be pearls, mixed with delicate foliage such as adiantum (Maidenhair fern). Fresh material which could be used includes symphoricarpus (snow-berries) – which looks exactly like pearls – and of course white tulips which have the right kind of irridescent sheen.

It might be fun to collect some oyster shells and to do individual arrangements in these, linked to the table centre with odd strings of pearls. A very pale pink or green cloth covered with white organza would give a suitable sort of effect.

35th – Coral

Another one which almost speaks for itself. Any flowers and leaves in shades of coral – particularly lucky if the anniversary is in the autumn because there are some beautiful coral-coloured dahlias and lots of leaves at this time; but roses and carnations come in the colour and are obtainable at other times. I suppose strings of coral beads went out years ago, but it is possible to find small pieces of coral which might be incorporated in the arrangement.

Pedestal in purple and reds for a Ruby wedding or a special occasion. Delphiniums, gladioli, stocks, carnations, roses etc

40th – Ruby
Lots of lovely deep red flowers – carnations, roses, dahlias, tulips – used with grey foliage if possible. Grey complements dark reds so much better than green, but it is a mistake to try to find red foliage. A dark colour like ruby red is apt to disappear, especially at night, so it needs a good background. If the container is to show, try to use red, grey, pewter or silver. These colours look lovely on a pale grey cloth and would be set off by red candles in silver candlesticks.

Plate 4
A pedestal for a Ruby wedding

50th – Golden

A very special one, and there is a tremendous variety of flowers in shades of gold at all seasons of the year.

It is not to be expected that gold containers are available, but again a tin of spray paint can work wonders. Use gold ribbon, baubles, even glitter, flowers made from gold foil – anything to create a really glamorous arrangement.

A white tablecloth is probably the best foil for this, and gold paper or plastic doilies can be used as bases and place mats. White candles with a gold '50' on them – the figures can be cut out and repeated again round the cloth. If a gold cloth is preferred, it is possible to spray a plastic cloth; but the figures will not show up on this unless they are sprinkled with a little gold glitter after they have been made.

For my own parents' golden wedding, I recreated my mother's bridal bouquet as far as possible and used a beautiful golden witch ball in the centre of the table flowers. I had some little plastic cherubs (which are in the shops at Christmas), so I sprayed these gold and attached them to the stem of a pair of very ordinary candlesticks.

It is also a good idea to have some containers ready for the flowers which are almost certain to arrive on the day. It is true that these are unlikely to have been well-conditioned, but I always feel that donors arriving at a party are rather pleased to see their gift prominently displayed. No-one is likely to have time to do much with late flowers; but perhaps if some cheap baskets were sprayed with gold beforehand and there was an oasis-filled tin at the ready, they could be quickly filled with whatever became available.

60th – Diamond

A rare and important celebration which calls for something very special. The haberdashery departments of most good stores can provide various things which could be used in a design for a diamond anniversary. Diamante and delicate diamond-like beads which can be strung on to stub wires and used between fresh flowers. These, too, need to be rather special – lilies-of-the-valley, for instance, which are now available throughout the year, and white heather. Anyone who celebrates 60 years of married life must deserve white heather!

There is a variety of plastic about which looks like pieces of glass; this could be piled in heaps to look like diamonds. Once again, many of the ideas suggested for the crystal anniversary could be used. Diamond-shaped place mats can be made by cutting thin cardboard and covering it with silver foil under clear plastic, or nylon. The table could be covered similarly. A liberal use of silver glitter can give a very diamond-like effect, too. Perhaps initials could be cut out, as a change from numbers, and silvered and glittered.

Simple Floristry

Let me say right away that a trained florist is undoubtedly the best person to make bouquets, etc. for special occasions and that it needs knowledge and practice to achieve the same results. Although it is not impossible to do some of the simpler things at home, it would be wise to try them out well in advance until some degree of skill is attained – or even to go to one of the floristry schools for a few basic lessons. It is also necessary for the amateur to have plenty of time available.

It is a good idea to experiment with several types of flowers before starting to make up anything. The remains of hyacinths are useful for practice; indeed, any fading flowers make good models and it doesn't matter if they get a bit mutilated.

I shall not attempt to describe any complicated methods but give simple instructions about mounting, wiring and making-up handsprays, corsages, buttonholes, a head-dress, a spray for a prayer book and a posy ball.

Material required: Stub wires 22 gauge (0·71mm) and 24 gauge (0·56mm); reel wire 32 gauge (0·24mm) and 36 gauge (0·20mm); florist's tape in white and green; ribbon; thin cardboard (for buttonholes); foam in foil or moss (for posy ball); basket; elastic (for head-dress)

First condition the flowers and foliage well, totally immersing ivy leaves and other foliage.

Mounting and wiring

This is absolutely essential for any floristry work, so do not be tempted to take any short cuts just because the flower has a good firm stem. It will not work. Wiring is to strengthen the stem of a flower and mounting is to provide a new stem. The natural stems are retained only on presentation sheafs, when the recipient may want to arrange the flowers herself afterwards.

The general principle is to keep all wired flowers and leaves as light as possible. The lower the gauge of wire, the thicker the wire, but the opposite applies in the metric system. The most useful sizes are those mentioned above. Different types of flowers need different techniques and it would not be possible to include all the various methods here. In general, I shall describe how to wire and mount roses, lily-of-the-valley, hyacinth pips and feathered carnations, with various leaves. I hope the reader will then be able to adapt the relevant method to whatever flower is to be used.

A finished bouquet

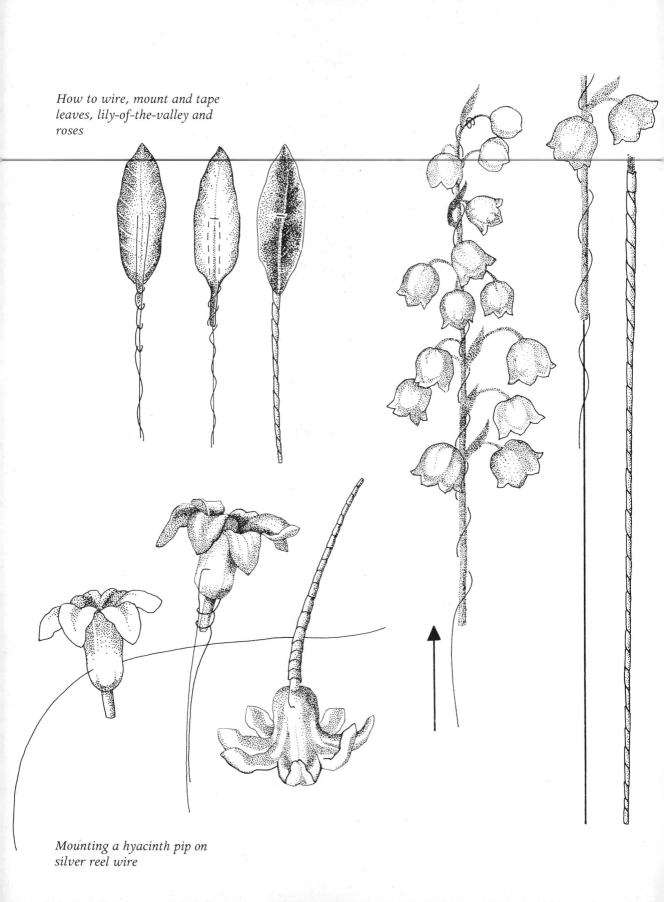

How to wire, mount and tape
leaves, lily-of-the-valley and
roses

Mounting a hyacinth pip on
silver reel wire

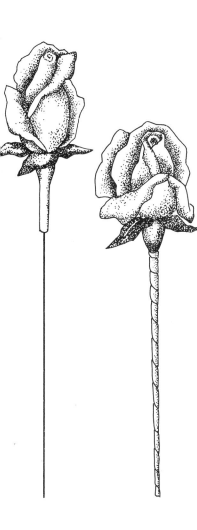

Roses

Cut the stem to about 1-in (2cm) and push a 0·71mm stub wire up through into the base of the flower. Then start to wind the tape around, starting from close up under the calyx so that the tiny piece of stem is incorporated. Start to wind at an angle and it will be found with practice that it is possible to hold the tape in one hand and the stem in the other and to twist the stem firmly so that the tape covers it tightly. Press the tape very firmly to itself after breaking it off at the end. If a rose is to be included in a flower ball, it may be wiser to use a stronger type of mounting – called double leg – by pushing the stub wire right through across the calyx, leaving one end longer than the other, and bending it down into a hairpin before taping it. Hold the bloom firmly as you do so.

Roses can be used in a 'cabbage' shape and this is made by using about five blooms. Take the petals off four and from the outside of the fifth, leaving the tight inside bud. Pleat each petal and wire them in groups and layers around the tight bud centre, using silver reel wire. This needs nimble fingers and patience!

Lily-of-the-valley

Very delicate flowers need a still lighter technique, and lily-of-the-valley should be wired with silver reel wire. Cut the stem to 1-in (2cm) below the bottom floret and start to wind the wire up through the florets. Finish at the top with a tiny hairpin of wire, then push a 24 gauge (0·56mm) stub wire into the stem before taping.

Hyacinths

Remove all the bells or pips from the flower; leave a tiny piece of stem if possible. Push a piece of reel wire about 7-in (18cm) long through the base of the pip, bend it into a hairpin shape with one end slightly longer than the other, then tape. It is wise to keep two fingers on the point where the wire is bent so that the flower does not tear. If 32 gauge (0·24mm) reel wire is used, it may not be necessary to add a stub wire, especially for a corsage.

Leaves

Single leaves from a rose or ivy leaves are very good for floristry work and are firm and long-lasting if conditioned well. Cut them with a tiny piece of stem, then thread the reel wire through the back of the leaf about one-third of the way up. Place a thumb on the point of insertion to prevent the leaf tearing and keep it there while the wire is bent down gently into a hairpin. Incorporate the piece of stem when winding the wire around, then tape. Leaves do not usually require extra stub wires as they are very light, but it may be necessary for bouquets.

Feathered carnations

Whole carnations are seldom used in floristry as they are too heavy for modern bouquets, but they are delightful – and economical – when taken to pieces and re-made. This is called feathering. Remove the sepals from underneath the flower and pull out all the petals, being careful not to break or damage them. Group three or four petals together and push a piece of reel wire through them about a quarter of the way up. Bend this down into a hairpin very carefully, so as not to break the petals, and with one end longer than the other. Wind the long end around the base of the petals and the other end of the wire, then tape.

Carnation buttonhole

It is not now so popular to include fern with a buttonhole but of course this is again a matter of taste. Certainly, a simple flower is much neater.

Cut the stem to about half-an-inch (1cm). Remove the seed pod from inside the flower by probing gently into the centre with finger and thumb. The pod can be felt and pulled away. Cut a small white disc from thin cardboard, about the size of an eggcup and cut a cross in the centre of this, being careful not to cut through to the edges. Remove the green sepals from beneath the flower then thread the disc onto the stem and push it right up as tightly as possible, underneath the bloom. Now push a 22 gauge (0·71mm) wire just below the cardboard circle but as tight up to the flower as possible. Push a second stub wire through at right angles to the first; now bend both wires down into a hairpin in line with the piece of natural stem. Cut to the length required and tape neatly.

A 'Malmaison' carnation, suitable for a lady, can be made in a similar way, but using two blooms together.

Corsages

Material required: About nine small leaves (they need not be all the same); three small roses (Carole are good); about ten hyacinth pips; about six pieces of feathered carnation, all wired and taped; reel wire; ribbon; tape

Start with one of the smallest pointed leaves and place a hyacinth pip in front of it and slightly lower. Start to bind them together, not too near the tip, with silver reel wire 36 gauge (0·20mm). Make about two turns before moving down the stem and incorporating the next item. Give each stem enough room for it to be moved later if required. Now begin to place some stems slightly to the side and to make them just a little longer. Do not forget to put in a leaf now and then and use the larger flowers, roses for instance, in a staggered line almost at the end; but leave one rose and a leaf for what is called the return end. This means that these two items are turned the opposite way from the rest of the flowers. It will be possible to adjust the shape of the spray after it is wired together and to bring

Stages in feathering a carnation

some of the flowers out to the side with a nice curve. This is the whole point of wiring every flower.

Now cut the wires evenly before taping right down, over the end and back again. Make sure the wires are all well covered otherwise a nasty stain can be left on a dress. It is usual to use green tape for corsages.

Bride's bouquet

Material required: Reel wire; white tape; white ribbon; white tissue paper; about 8 leaves, different shapes; about 12 sprays Lily-of-the-valley; about 12 pieces of feathered carnations; about 10 hyacinth pips; three small rosebuds; six small roses; all wired, mounted and taped

Do try to get the size of the bouquet right in proportion to the bride. Persuade a small girl not to have a tight round posy with too many flowers; and, equally, avoid a tiny spray for someone tall. The shower bouquet described here can be made as large or as small as required by varying the size and amount of material used. It can also be curved to either side when finished or left straight.

Take a small pointed leaf, place a lily-of-the-valley spray in front and a little below and bind firmly together with reel wire, about two turns. Move downwards with each of the next five stems, using slightly larger flowers and leaves towards the centre. Now start to lengthen the stems a little and to place some at the sides; leave enough room on each to be able to curve the stem outwards. Keep one rosebud and about ten other pieces, including leaves, to make the return end later. This is where the bouquet is bent to make it easier to hold. Do not twist the stub wires around each other, unless the flower is specially heavy. This twisting makes the bouquet a little clumsy and must be avoided if possible, though sometimes it is necessary in order to anchor a flower and prevent it moving out of place. Continue downwards, with each stem a tiny bit longer than the last one, until 40 pieces have been used, with the largest rose at the bottom centre. The last two or three pieces, including the rose, should be bent at right angles to the main stem, and the bottom side stems will be the maximum width. Now bend the mass of wires right down into a hairpin shape to make the handle. Try placing another small pointed leaf along this bend, facing away from the main flowers, to determine the final length. Fill up the space between this and the central flowers with the pieces put by, remembering to graduate the sizes towards the centre again.

Now cut the wires off neatly and cut a strip of tissue paper. Bind this thoroughly around all the wires, up to the cut ends and back, rather like a bandage, so that everything is well covered in. A rusty wire could ruin a lovely dress, remember. Fix the end with sticky tape, then cover it all again with white ribbon. Streamers and a bow of ribbon may be added if desired, also fixed with sticky tape.

TOP *Starting to make a bouquet; the first flowers wired together*
BOTTOM *Ready to start return end and before the handle is bent*

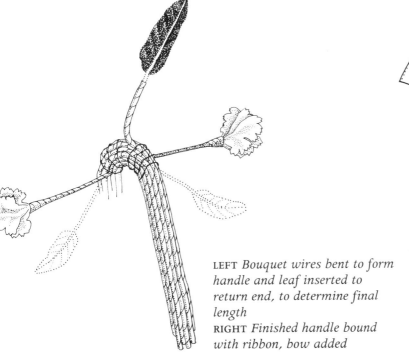

LEFT *Bouquet wires bent to form handle and leaf inserted to return end, to determine final length*
RIGHT *Finished handle bound with ribbon, bow added*

Spray for a prayer book

Follow the instructions for making a corsage, then fold a piece of white ribbon in half (about 2-in (5cm) wide and about 20-in (50cm) long plus twice the length of the book). Insert it in the page with the marriage service and out over the front cover. Cut the ends at an angle and catch the ribbon together just underneath the edge of the book. The spray, when completed, may be curved slightly or left quite straight before attaching it to the ribbon on the front of the book, either by sticky tape, or by the safer method of sewing it to the ribbon. Make the spray in proportion to the size of the book, of course. This spray could also be used on a small handbag.

Head-dress

Material required: Ten or more leaves; ten feathered carnations; ten hyacinth pips, or freesias; three to five roses, graduating in size; all wired and mounted on reel wire, leaving long pieces, but not taped; two 22 gauge (0·71mm) stub wires; elastic

Take the two stub wires and mould them across the head, making a half-circle. Cover with brown tape, then turn back a small loop at both ends – this should come just above the ears – and bind this with reel wire. Fix a length of elastic through the loops, again fitting it to the head which is to wear it, and stitch it firmly in place.

Divide the flowers and leaves into two, plus the largest rose for the centre. Make a small mark in the exact centre of the wire band because it is very easy to lose this and to get the head-dress unbalanced.

Start at one end with a pointed leaf facing away from the centre, wire this on to hide the side loop. If enough wire has been left on each piece it will not be necessary to use extra wire; the legs of wire can be cut away as you go along. It must be kept tidy at the back or the wires will stick into the poor girl's head! After the first leaf, work towards the centre, using larger flowers each time until half have been used. Then start at the other end and repeat the process. Place the large rose in the centre and fill in on either side of this.

Becareful that the circlet does not twist as you work. The head-dress can be used in various ways – as an Alice band, a back spray or made into a full circle (no elastic needed for the last three). Hairpins inserted through the loops give added security.

A bridesmaid's posy ball

Material required: Sphagnum moss or damp foam wrapped in silver foil; 20 feathered carnations; 20 small roses; 20 chrysanthemum florets; ribbon; stub wires; reel wire. All mounted on short stub wires, not taped

This type of moss can be found in many woods, but if it is not possible to get it, a ball of foam, well-soaked and wrapped in foil will do. When using moss, press it into a small well-rounded ball, not too tight, and bind it round with reel wire, taking it all over several times. Make a loop of ribbon, in a colur to tone with the flowers, and attach the ends firmly to the middle of a strong stub wire. Bend the wire in half, push both pieces right through the ball and bend them back again. Do make sure that the mechanics of a ball are secure; many little bridesmaids swing them round like real balls so they could come apart very easily.

Now there is a loop to form a handle, and the ball can be suspended while the flowers are being inserted. Cut most of the wires on the flowers to just a little less than the diameter of the ball and push them home very firmly. The wires of the flowers underneath should be pushed right through the ball. It is best to wire the rose by the method mentioned earlier in the instructions about this flower. Make sure that all the foundation of the ball is covered. A few extra pieces of ribbon, double or single and quite short, can now be added around the ribbon loop of the handle.

LEFT *Small bouquet of chrysanthemums, lily-of-the-valley, heather, feathered carnations and ivy leaves*
CENTRE *Bridesmaid's ball made from marguerites*
RIGHT *Wiring a carnation buttonhole*

More Ideas

A home-made container

Material required: A large solid circle about 12-in (30cm) in diameter and half-an-inch (1cm) thick; a rounded block of wood about 9-in (23cm) long and 3-in (8cm) in diameter; three pieces of plastic scroll (the kind which is used to decorate glass doors and comes from a D.I.Y. shop); three plastic cherubs about 5-in (13cm) high; tin for top

Screw the block of wood to the flat base and the tin on top of the block (as a container). Fix the scrolls at even intervals around the sides of the block, at right angles, with the cherubs in between. Now spray the whole article. I use a mixture, putting gold on top of silver while still wet, to obtain a very attractive effect.

Colour

Try matching colours of food and decorations – not as mad as it may sound! Harmless vegetable dye or a clever choice will cope with the food. Say lots of green salads for a garden lunch, cucumber mousse, melon, etc., with green and white flowers. Why not? Fun and a talking point anyway.

Using feathers

Material required: Various feathers (the most easily obtainable are of course from chickens, but get a variation if possible); Dylon dye; reel wire; stub wire; florist's tape; beads; smaller feathers (or anything suitable to make stamens); yoghurt or cream pot; plaster mixture; paint

I have made a delightful feather tree with ordinary white chicken feathers, but they can be dyed any colour required. Use a hot water Dylon dye and dip the feathers in – very briefly for a delicate colour and longer for a more vivid shade. Do not be dismayed at the bedraggled result. Spread them out to dry and they will be perfectly all right.

To make a tree, gather together three, four or five feathers according to the size of the tree. It is best to start at the top of the tree with small bunches and increase the size towards the base. Bind each group tightly together with reel or fuse wire, then mount this on a long stub wire. Cover with tape. Make about 18 of these, then bind them together in the shape of a tree (as described under 'Plastic Trees').

A 'tree' made from white chicken feathers, hung with beads

Feather flowers

Take about eight feathers and group them around whatever has been chosen to make a centre. Small beads on wires, a group of different small feathers, a tiny seed-head or a small bauble will be suitable. Wire the group together, then mount and tape. Green or brown tape will simulate a stem.

These flowers can be used to make a spray. I usually take about seven for the flower and three or four green groups (without centres) for leaves, for the largest sprays. Keep a natural formation in mind when making these – small leaves and flowers at the top and working downwards at about one inch (2cm) intervals. Bind them together with tape to the end of the stub wires, which should provide a fairly long stem.

Two or three of these sprays, grouped with nice curves into an Oriental-style arrangement, look most effective and are so useful when flowers are scarce. They can be gently washed and dried to put away until required again.

Baroque-style candle-holders

Material required: Any ordinary candle-stick; two round beer mats; tiny baubles; bows; dried seed-heads; beads; paint; glitter; glue; candle

Glue the beer mats together, then put them on top of the candle-stick, making a hole for the candle. Glue all the remaining material all over the mat and around the candle; then spray gold or silver (protecting the candle itself).

Stars

Ordinary polystyrene ceiling tiles can be cut into star shapes and hung, or used as a centre-piece for an arrangement.

Inserting a candle into an arrangement

Take three pieces of strong stub wire, each about 5-in (13cm) long, bend them into hairpin shapes and attach them around the base of the candle with sticky tape, allowing the prongs to project for half their length at the base. These can be inserted, quite easily, into foam or a pinholder and will stay firmly in place without the need to make a large hole.

Using old wine bottles

Many bottle shapes are attractive, but clear glass looks rather ordinary for party use. Fill the bottle with water (which will also give it better balance), then colour the water with ordinary vegetable colouring according to the colour scheme required. Replace the cork and attach a container which is specially designed for bottles or, if the arrangement is to be dried or plastic, a wedge of plasticine.

Sprays of flowers made from dyed chicken feathers

Honesty tree

Material required: Branch; seed-heads of honesty; thread; dull white paint; glue; glitter

Look for a good heavy tree branch, well shaped. Fasten it firmly either to a heavy pin-holder or to a weighted plaster base. Whiten the branch and base. Remove the seed-heads from some sprays of honesty and thread each one on very thin thread (black shows least of all). Dip the edges of the honesty in colourless glue, then in glitter before hanging them, at irregular intervals, from the branches. This tree can also be made with white feathers instead of honesty, or with baubles or glittery beads.

Tubes for pedestals

To avoid buying too many florist's tubes for a pedestal, collect those firm little foil tubes from cigars. Tape these to thin sticks and paint green.

Extra material for arranging

Cover some fairly firm stub wires with gold or silver paint, glitter ribbon or tinsel. Then roll the wire around a small stick, pencil or thick knitting needle. This will produce a very delicate spiral to place between straighter material in an arrangement.

Hanging christmas cards

I suppose we all like to get the Christmas cards away from a flat surface, where they must be moved every time the room is dusted. I buy coloured sticky tape and pin strips of this on the walls, sticky side out. It is then very quick to just push the card on to the tape. I recommend that the roll is left attached to the strip until this is full, otherwise it may curl up and get into a tangle.

Freezing flowers

One way of adding some inexpensive glamour to a winter arrangement (if there is a freezer available) is to deep-freeze some roses in the summer.

Pick buds showing some colour and condition them well, removing most of the foliage. Place the stems in a shallow plastic container as long as possible and about half cover them with water. Put them in the freezer for an hour or so until they are just embedded in ice, then cover with more water and fully freeze them. When wanted for use, allow them to thaw out at room temperature and arrange immediately. The flowers will open quickly and are not likely to last long; but it is fun to have garden roses in the middle of winter.

Another idea is to put full-blown stemless roses in separate plastic containers (yoghurt or cream pots), face downwards; cover with water, add the lid and freeze completely. For a party, put a small bowl at each place, take out the container and dip it in hot water just enough to loosen the blooms. Then slide them into the bowls, face upwards. At the beginning of the meal, these roses are completely enclosed in a beautiful crystal-like covering which melts gently through the evening, releasing not only an exquisite flower but providing ready-filled finger bowls as well.

Flowers as gifts

Of course, any flowers are acceptable as gifts, but how much nicer if they are already arranged. A busy hostess seldom has time, either just before or during a party, to arrange flowers; and it is as nice for the recipient as for the giver to be able to enjoy them immediately. Any kind of arrangement can be made to look festive by the addition of some ribbon bows, but there are other ideas which also give that little extra lift to a present.

If it is to go to a man and a woman, try putting one really lovely rose – or even an orchid – inside a brandy glass so that there is something for both. A house-proud girl might like to get one of the useful straight-sided storage jars; put a small pinholder at the base of this and impale a rose on it. Any kind of wine glass can be pressed into service for this type of gift. If it is difficult to get the flower onto the base, bind it to a small stick and impale this on the pinholder. Small bunches of snowdrops, primroses or violets look charming done this way.

A more elaborate and lasting gift is a *pot et fleur,* which consists of plants and cut flowers in one container. All kinds of things can be used as the container – copper or brass bowls, large old-fashioned wash-hand basins, boxes, baskets or simply a bulb bowl. Choose plants which need similar treatment and will live happily together, and vary the height and the textures. It is usually best to put the plants directly into a compost mixture. If there are any which are 'difficult' plants (begonia rex, for instance, which does not like to be over-watered from the top), these can be put into plastic bags filled with moist compost and then removed when the remainder are being watered.

An evening bag and a parcel decorated with a fresh orchid, attached with sticky tape

I use a sansevieria (mother-in-law's tongue) for height, chloro-

phytum (spider plant) and tradescantia, with one of the indoor ivies trailing over the edge. If a well-soaked piece of oasis is placed in between the plants, a few flowers can be inserted in this and easily removed or replaced at any time. Add a large bow in the flower colours – and there is a magnificent and lasting gift.

For hospital gifts, I make small cones stuffed with wet foam and lined with foil. These last a long time, take up little room and give no bother to the nurses. I often use a foil case (I wash and store all the foil containers after we have eaten the contents!) with wet oasis secured inside with a strip of sticky tape. Fix the tape over the oasis before damping it or the tape will not adhere. This is then an expendable container.

Miniature bottles of liqueurs can make pretty and unusual containers, too. A piece of damp, foil-wrapped oasis can be wired to the top or side and needs only a few delicate flowers and some foliage. I have found a ball of flowers an acceptable hospital gift. There is usually somewhere it can hang, and I have described this under 'Flowers for Bridesmaids'.

Fruit and flowers can be combined to make an acceptable and attractive present. One idea is to insert a ring of small flowers around a pineapple. Or to attach a bunch of grapes to a flower-filled container.

Flowers and vegetables
In France, where basic ingredients for cooking are taken most seriously, I have seen many striking arrangements which combine flowers with fruit, vegetables and herbs.

Built up on a pyramid of foam or wire netting, it is possible to mix artichokes, carrots with their own foliage, beautifully washed sticks of celery, parsley going to seed, sprays of nuts fresh from the hedgerow, all kinds of herbs – in fact, anything which is to hand. These all look fine even without flowers and are specially suitable for an informal party. As it is unlikely that the guests will eat them, the thrifty cook can use them afterwards. And it is a very useful idea for a quick decoration or when flowers are scarce.

Nylon flowers
Save old nylon stockings or tights, ones as fine as possible. Shape a piece of stub wire, about 28 gauge (0·38mm) into a petal, pull the nylon rightly around it and bind with reel wire. Using beads, seed-heads (beech masts look very good) as a centre stamen, mounted on a stronger stub wire, group four or five petals around into a flower shape. Neaten the stem with florist's tape.

These dull-surfaced flowers, in muted colours, look most unusual with a dried arrangement or mixed with gold at Christmas, when the stamen could also be gilded.

Net trees

Basic foundation is made as described in 'Pot Trees' by inserting a stick into a yoghurt pot; but this time the stick is decorated with layers of net, rather like a ballet dress.

An average size tree takes about one-and-a-half yards (metres) of nylon net and this is cut into four pieces: 4-in (10cm), 8-in (20cm), 12-in (30cm), and 16-in (40cm) wide. Gather one edge of each piece using strong thread and pull up tightly to fit around the stick; then place them firmly around the stick, starting with the widest layer at the base. The stick can also be painted to match and the net decorated with tiny beads, pearls or baubles.

Red, white or green net looks Christmassy; and pale pinks, blues or pastel colours would be suitable for other parties.

A pyramid of variegated flowers for a party